1001 Teaching Tips

Helpful Hints for Working With Young Children

Compiled by the Totline Staff
Illustrated by Gary Mohrmann

Totline® Publications
A Division of Frank Schaffer Publications, Inc.
Torrance, California

We wish to thank the teachers, parents and childcare workers whose names appear on pages 206–207 for contributing so many of their favorite teaching tips to this book.

Editorial Staff:
   Editorial Manager: Kathleen Cubley
   Editors: Gayle Bittinger, Elizabeth McKinnon, Jean Warren
   Copy Editor: Brenda Mann Harrison
   Indexer: Miriam Bulmer
   Proofreader: Kris Fulsaas
   Editorial Assistant: Erica West

Design and Production Staff:
   Art Manager: Jill Lustig
   Book Design/Layout: Sarah Ness
   Cover: Eric Stovall
   Cover Illustration: Larry Countryman
   Production Manager: Jo Anna Brock

ISBN 0-911019-64-2

Library of Congress Catalog Number 93-60118
Printed in the United States of America
Published by: Totline® Publications

Business Office: 23740 Hawthorne Blvd.
            Torrance, CA 90505

Introduction

Busy teachers on limited budgets need all the help they can get.

That's why we at Warren Publishing House have combined our best ideas with those submitted by the readers of the *Totline*™ newsletter to bring you these 1001 shortcuts to success.

1001 Teaching Tips is divided into three sections; Curriculum Tips, Room Tips, and Special Times Tips. As you glance through the book, you will find tips for art, language, and science times; tips for decorating your room, organizing materials, and making administrative chores easier; tips for field trips, holidays, and transition times—plus much, much more.

To make this resource book easy to use, we arranged the contents alphabetically and added a subject index at the back of the book to help you locate a particular tip quickly.

Teachers helping teachers is what this book is all about. The tips included were found by their contributors to be inexpensive, easy, and appropriate for them. Keep in mind that when working with young children, it is always advisable to test new ideas before using them with children.

Many of the tips in this book were taken from the Warren Publishing House book *Teaching Tips*, which is now out of print.

We hope that you will find *1001 Teaching Tips* to be a useful, handy resource. Our motto is spend less and have *more*—more time for children, more inexpensive supplies, more fun!

Contents

ROOM TIPS

SPECIAL TIMES TIPS

CURRICULUM TIPS

Art Tips

Crayons

Better Crayon Use

1 Remove the paper from crayons before handing them out. Your children will use more of the crayon.

Big Crayons

2 Provide your children with large crayons to use for drawing and coloring. The big crayons are easier for young children to control.

Preventing Crayon Breaks

3 New crayons won't break as easily if you wrap them with masking tape before letting your children use them.

Using Old Crayons

4 Peel the paper off all your old crayons at the end of the school year. They can be used the following year for art projects that require coloring with the sides of crayons.

Molded Crayons

5 Mold old crayons into new shapes. Melt broken pieces of the crayons in disposable pans, then pour the liquid into small plastic molds. Chill in a refrigerator for easy removal.

Crayon Keepers

6 Powdered formula cans with lids make perfect crayon keepers. Sort crayons into the cans by color. Then cover each can with a matching color of construction paper.

Bandage Box Holder

7 A metal bandage box with a hinged lid is great for holding crayons.

Felt-Tip Markers

Avoiding Marker Mix-Ups

8 When purchasing felt-tip markers for your room, select two separate brands: one for permanent markers for making posters and games and one for water-based markers for your children to use. This makes it easy to avoid giving your children permanent markers by mistake.

Felt-Tip Marker Holder

9 Felt-tip markers can dry out fast if their caps get lost. Solve the problem by placing the caps, open ends up, in a clean whipped-topping tub filled with plaster of Paris. (Make sure that the plaster does not run down into the caps.) When the plaster dries around the caps, the markers can be put back into the caps and will stand upright until you are ready to use them again.

Rejuvenating Felt-Tip Markers

10 When felt-tip markers dry out, put drops of water inside the caps. Then store the markers tip side down with the caps on.

Recycling Felt-Tip Markers

11 Recycle dried-out felt-tip markers by letting your children dip them into paint and use them for creative drawing.

Finger Painting

Painting on Freezer Wrap

12 Freezer wrap (the kind with one coated side) is great for finger painting. It comes in large rolls, won't tear when wet, and is relatively inexpensive.

Painting on Wrapping Paper

13 When your supply of finger-paint paper runs out, a good substitute is white glossy wrapping paper, either new or used.

Painting on Shelf Paper

14 Let your children finger-paint on white shelf paper that has been cut into large pieces.

Fence Me In

15 When a child is finger-painting directly on a table, keep paint contained in a desired area by making a "fence" on the tabletop with strips of masking tape. Ask the child to paint inside the fence.

Finger-Painted Prints

16 To eliminate torn papers and facilitate cleanup when finger-painting, try this. Let your children finger-paint directly on plastic trays. When each child finishes, lay a piece of construction paper on top of his or her design and rub across it with your hand. Lift the paper from the tray to reveal the child's finger-painted print. Following the activity, rinse off the trays in a sink.

Stand Up and Paint

17 To encourage freedom of movement, have your children stand rather than sit when they are finger-painting.

Painting in Highchairs

18 Very young children can enjoy finger painting while sitting in highchairs. There's no need for paper—the children can paint directly on the high-chair trays. Painting with pudding is a real favorite.

Cleanup Fun

19 After your children have been finger-painting, squirt shaving cream on the table for them to play with. This will help clean their hands and the table-top at the same time.

Washing Up

20 If you need an extra sink when your children are finger-painting, fill your water table with warm, soapy water and let the children use it for washing their hands.

Finger-Painted Papers

21 Finger-painting on cut-out shapes can be difficult for young children. Instead, have them paint on large paper squares, then cut the squares into desired shapes when the paint has dried.

Finger Paints

Shaving Cream

22 Squirt shaving cream on a tabletop and let your children finger-paint with it. Cleanup is quick, leaving table and hands squeaky clean.

Colored Shaving Cream

23 Make finger painting with shaving cream more interesting by adding drops of food coloring.

Quick Finger Paints

24 Let your children finger-paint with liquid starch or a mixture of Ivory Snow soap powder and water. Add drops of food coloring or tempera paint for color.

Hand Lotion

25 Pour white or colorless hand lotion into a bowl and stir in a drop or two of food coloring. The lotion makes a fun finger paint that is easy on little hands.

Homemade Finger Paint

26 For an easy-to-make, economical finger paint, mix until smooth 2 tablespoons cornstarch and 2 table-spoons cold water. Add 1 cup boiling water and stir until smooth again. For color, add powdered tempera paint or drops of food coloring.

Edible Finger Paints

27 For finger paints that are both fun and tasty, let your children use instant pudding, whipped cream or yogurt.

Corn Syrup

28 Light corn syrup makes a great finger paint that leaves a shiny finish when dry. Let your children finger-paint with plain corn syrup on colored construction paper. Or add drops of food coloring to syrup for finger-painting on white paper.

Finger-Paint Pumps

29 Save liquid soap pump bottles (or buy pump bottles at a pharmacy) and fill them with finger paint. The bottles help distribute the right amount of paint for little hands to use.

Glitter

Glitter Dispensers

30 Use baby food jars to make glitter dispensers. Punch holes in the lids. Then fill the jars with glitter and put the lids back on securely.

Regulating Sprinkles

31 Before your children use a glitter dispenser with a perforated lid, cover a few of the holes with transparent tape to prevent over-sprinkling.

Glitter Savers

32 When your children are gluing glitter on artwork, have them first place their artwork in shallow box lids. After they sprinkle on the glitter, the excess can be tapped off into the box lids and saved for other projects.

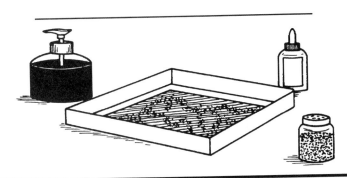

No-Mess Glitter

33 Here's an easy way for your children to apply glitter to artwork. Just mix the glitter with glue for them to brush on their papers. You'll have sparkle without the mess!

Glitter Substitute

34 Add drops of food coloring to salt. Stir well and allow the salt to dry. Store in shaker containers. The colored salt is great for sprinkling over glue to add sparkle or texture, and it's less expensive than glitter.

Glue

Glue Extender

35 If you mix a little water with white glue, it will last longer while still doing its job.

Homemade Glue Recipe

36 ½ cup cornstarch, divided
1½ cups water, divided
2 tablespoons light corn syrup
1 teaspoon white vinegar

In a saucepan, combine ¼ cup cornstarch, ¾ cup water, corn syrup and vinegar. Cook over medium heat, stirring constantly, until the mixture thickens. In a separate bowl, combine until smooth the remaining ¼ cup cornstarch and ¾ cup water. Slowly add this mixture to the hot mixture in the pan and stir until well mixed. Store glue up to 2 months in a covered container.

Colored Glue

37 Instead of buying expensive colored glue, simply mix drops of food coloring with white glue and refill your empty bottles.

Craft Stick Applicators

38 Let your children use craft sticks or small pieces of wood to spread glue.

Foam Paintbrush Applicators

39 Foam-rubber paintbrushes (available in paint and hardware stores) are great for spreading glue over large areas.

Cotton Swab Applicators

40 To help your children apply glue evenly, give them cotton swabs. The swabs are easy to hold and work well for gluing small items.

Glue Squares

41 When you don't have enough glue bottles to go around, squeeze a small glue puddle on a square of paper for each child. The children can use one of their fingers or a cotton swab to apply the glue. Simply throw the squares away when they finish.

Glue Substitutes

42 When very young children are making paper collages, let them use cold cream, petroleum jelly or other thick, nontoxic ointments as glue substitutes.

Edible Glue

43 Let your children use peanut butter as glue when creating sculptures with food items such as crackers or pretzels.

Glue Containers

Glue Bottles

44 Have each child bring an 8-ounce bottle of glue to keep at school as part of his or her supplies. Transfer the glue into 1¼-ounce bottles for the children to use during art activities. The small bottles are easy for the children to handle and can be refilled throughout the school year.

Squeeze Bottles

45 Purchase small, plastic squeeze bottles with caps from a drugstore. The bottles can be filled with glue to make individual dispensers for your children.

Jar Lids

46 Use jar lids for individual glue containers during art activities.

Glue Cups

47 Use disposable condiment cups, cream cups or communion cups for individual glue containers.

No More Stuck Caps

48 To prevent the caps of glue containers from sticking shut, wipe a thick coat of petroleum jelly on the threads of the caps the first time the containers are opened.

Keeping Things Clean

Plastic Tablecloth Cover

49 Cover a work area with an old plastic tablecloth for easy cleanup after projects that require paint, sand, glitter or water. Just shake out the cloth or wipe it clean with a damp sponge.

Plastic Shower Curtains

50 Ask parents to donate old plastic shower curtains. These can be used as floor coverings for water, paint and sand projects or as table coverings for painting, gluing or using clay.

Easel Area

51 Mark off a square area around your painting easel by attaching electrical tape to the floor. Have your children keep the area covered with newspaper to catch spills when painting. When they finish, have them toss the newspaper into a recycling bin.

Paper Scrap Bag

52 For easy cleanup after a cutting project, tape an open grocery bag to one end of the art table. When the children finish working, they can sweep the scraps off the table into the bag.

Clean Paint

53 Adding a small amount of liquid dishwashing detergent or liquid hand soap to tempera paint makes it easy to wipe up spills and to wash paint out of clothing.

Using Disposables

54 Make cleanup a breeze by using yogurt containers, plastic-foam food trays and other common household disposables for holding art materials while your children are working. At the conclusion of art time, throw out the disposables.

Paint Pot Throwaways

55 Try lining the insides of your paint pots with plastic bags before you fill them. At the end of the day or week, throw the bags away and insert new ones.

Preventing Water Spills

56 Instead of having your children fill their own water containers during painting activities, try this. Provide each child with an empty container. Then walk around the art table and fill each container from a pitcher of water. This helps prevent spills.

Quick Art Smocks

57 Let your children wear old, adult-size T-shirts for art smocks. The shirts cover clothes nicely and can be tossed into a washer after each use.

Waterproof Smocks

58 Use clean, old plastic shower curtains to make painting smocks. For each smock, cut out a rectangle measuring 18 by 36 inches. Fold it in half to make an 18-inch square and cut a head hole along the fold. Then staple the sides together, leaving room at the top for armholes.

Making Prints

Potato Stamp

59 To make carving a design in a potato half easier, try this. Choose a small cookie cutter with a desired shape and push it down into the cut end of the potato. Then carve the potato away from the outside edges of the cookie cutter. Remove the cookie cutter and you'll have a raised, cut-out shape for making prints.

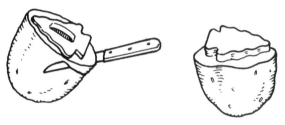

Printing With Silk Leaves

60 When real leaves are not available for making prints, try using silk leaves (available where artificial flowers are sold). Have your children brush paint on the front sides of the silk leaves and then press the leaves on paper.

Sponge Stamps

61 Cut thin sponges into hearts, squares or other shapes that are about 2½ inches across. Make a handle for each sponge shape by hot-gluing it to the bottom of a plastic film container. This will make sponge painting much easier for little hands.

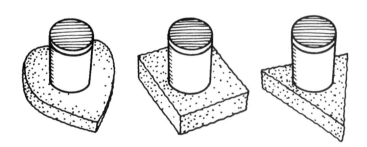

Pasta Stamps

62 Uncooked pasta shapes, such as wheels or shells, can be used to make printing stamps. Glue the shapes on wood blocks, thread spools or corks. To prevent the pasta shapes from breaking, have your children put paper towels underneath their papers when making prints.

Insole Stamps

63 Here's an easy way to make stamps. Cut small shapes out of shoe insoles (available at drugstores) and glue them on wood blocks. Use the stamps with commercial ink pads to make prints.

Building Block Stamps

64 Let your children dip square, rectangular or cylindrical building blocks into paint and press them on paper to make prints.

Printing With Puzzle Pieces

65 Use commercial foam-rubber puzzle pieces for sponge-printing projects. Let your children dip the pieces into paint and then press them on paper.

Making Rubbings

Embossed Greeting Cards

66 Let your children place paper on top of embossed greeting cards and color over the raised designs with crayons to make rubbings.

Sticker Sheet Rubbings

67 After peeling stars, hearts or other stickers from their backings, give the empty sticker sheets to your children to use for making rubbings.

Leaf Rubbings

68 When making leaf rubbings, place dabs of plastic adhesive on the backs of the leaves to help them stick to the art table. Plastic adhesive is sold in office-supply stores for hanging posters and other lightweight materials.

Tape Loops

69 To make rubbings of coins, cardboard letters, etc., first attach the items to a tabletop with loops of masking tape rolled sticky side out. Or use double-stick tape to keep the items from sliding around.

Paint Containers

Squeeze Bottle Storage

70 Pour tempera paint into plastic squeeze bottles with caps for easy storage.

Shampoo Bottles

71 Use squirt-top shampoo bottles to store and dispense tempera paint. Clear-plastic bottles work especially well, allowing you to see the paint colors at a glance.

Milk Cartons

72 Cut milk cartons down to make containers for tempera paint.

Laundry Soap Caps

73 Save the large caps from bottles of liquid laundry detergent. Your children can use the caps for paint holders during art activities.

Yogurt Cups

74 Use yogurt cups with lids to make paint holders. Cut a small circle in the lid of each cup for inserting a paintbrush. The lids help to scrape off excess paint and slow down spills if holders are dropped.

Ash Trays

75 Look for old ash trays with grooves in the sides to use as paint holders. Small paintbrushes can rest in the grooves and won't tip over.

Plastic-Foam Trays

76 Let your children use plastic-foam food trays as paint holders during art activities. If desired, cut shallow grooves in the sides of the trays for holding paintbrushes.

Divided Dish

77 When you need a container for holding several different colors of paint at one time, try using a plastic dish that is divided into sections (the kind used for feeding infants).

Paint Tote

78 Use baby food jars with lids as paint containers. Store the jars in a cardboard soft-drink carrier for easy toting.

Paint Trays

79 Save the sturdy, thick-cardboard beverage trays from fast-food restaurants. Use the trays for storing and carrying paint containers such as yogurt cups or baby food jars. To prevent spills, make sure the paint containers have lids.

Sauce Bottles

80 Pour paint into glass sauce bottles that have plastic drip-control inserts in the tops. Let your children use the bottles for drip-painting projects.

Glue Bottles

81 Fill empty glue bottles with paint. Then open the screw-on caps partway and let your children dribble the paint onto paper.

Opening Paint Jars

82 Removing a too-tight lid from a paint jar can be difficult. Slip a rubber dishwashing glove on your hand first and it will be easier to unscrew the lid.

Paintbrushes

Foam-Rubber Brushes

83 Foam-rubber brushes (available at paint stores) are great for painting projects. The brushes come in various sizes and are relatively inexpensive.

Clothespin Paintbrushes

84 Clip spring-type clothespins to cotton balls, sponge pieces or small squares of felt to make paintbrushes. The clothespin handles will keep little hands clean while painting.

Mini-Paintbrushes

85 For tiny paintbrushes with easy-to-grasp handles, use old nail polish caps with attached brushes. Rinse first in nail polish remover, then wash the caps and brushes thoroughly in warm, soapy water. (Work in an area away from children when using nail polish remover.)

Spoons

86 For a different kind of art experience, let your children use spoons to spread paint on paper.

Nature Items

87 Look for nature items that can be used as paintbrushes. Try feathers, twigs, dried grasses or dried flowers.

Paintbrush Holder

88 Tape together several pairs of cardboard toilet-tissue tubes. Use six to make a six-pack, eight to make an eight-pack, etc. Stand the tubes upright in an open shoe box or a facial tissue box that has the top cut off. Use the tubes for sorting and storing different sizes of paintbrushes.

Paints

Painting on Slick Surfaces

89 To make paint that will adhere to slick surfaces, such as plastic-foam or waxed milk cartons, mix powdered tempera with liquid hand soap until paint is the desired consistency.

Painting on Foil

90 For painting on foil, use a mixture of two-thirds liquid tempera to one-third liquid dishwashing detergent. A light coating of hairspray over the painting will add gloss and help prevent chipping. (Work in an area away from children when using hairspray.)

Oh-So-Smooth Paint

91 For extra-smooth paint, try mixing powdered tempera and water in a blender.

Paint Thickener

92 To cut down on drips, use liquid starch to thicken easel paint and paint used for murals.

Dripless Paint

93 Here's an easy way to make your own dripless paint. Combine ¾ cup cornstarch with cold water to make a thick, smooth paste. Stir in boiling water until the mixture is the desired consistency. For color, add powdered tempera paint.

No More Chips

94 When painting large boxes or murals, pour liquid dishwashing detergent into the paint. This will help prevent the paint from chipping off once it has dried.

Paint Extender

95 To extend paint, add a little Ivory Snow soap powder to powdered tempera before mixing it with water. This also makes it easier to wash any paint spills out of clothing.

Textured Paint

96 To add texture, try stirring used, rinsed coffee grounds into liquid tempera paint.

Glossy Paint

97 For glossy paint, mix powdered tempera with condensed milk instead of water.

Fresh Paints

98 A few drops of glycerin added to tempera paints will keep them fresh and sweet-smelling. Look for glycerin in drugstores.

Paint and Sniff

99 To deepen sensory learning, add drops of food flavoring to liquid tempera paints. Try lemon flavoring in yellow paint, mint in green, vanilla in white, and peppermint in red.

Homemade Watercolors

100 Here's an inexpensive way to make your own watercolor sets. Pour different colors of leftover tempera paint into plastic-foam egg-carton cups. Set them aside to dry and harden. The paints can be used with water and brushes, just like ordinary watercolors.

Sugar Paint

101 In a small bowl, mix 2 tablespoons white powdered tempera paint with ¼ cup white sugar. Spoon the mixture into a shaker container. Let your children sprinkle the sugar paint over glue brushed on black construction paper to make snow scenes.

Paste

Learning How to Paste

102 For young children, learning how to paste takes lots of practice. For their first experience, let them place pre-pasted shapes on paper. The next time, have them spread lumps of paste that you have applied. Finally, when they are ready, let the children apply and spread the paste, and place the shapes on paper themselves.

Pasting Paper Chains

103 When your children are first learning how to make paper chains, let them use strips cut from colorful pages of glossy magazines. The slick paper is easier to paste than construction paper.

No More Dry Paste

104 Paste stays moist longer if you keep a piece of damp sponge in the jar.

Playdough

Keeping It Soft

105 Keep playdough soft by storing it in an airtight container with a piece of damp cloth.

Textured Playdough

106 Try working a small amount of sand into playdough to add texture.

Glitter Playdough

107 For special occasions, sprinkle glitter on a tabletop and let your children work it into pieces of playdough.

Scented Playdough

108 Add scents to playdough by working in drops of food flavoring. Try matching scents with colors—mint with green, lemon with yellow, or chocolate with brown.

Coloring Playdough

109 To make homemade playdough with vivid color, use powdered tempera paint instead of food coloring. (This works best for older children, who are not likely to put the playdough into their mouths.)

Tasty Playdough Substitutes

110 It won't matter if your children put their masterpieces in their mouths if you let them use pie dough or thawed bread dough as playdough substitutes.

Playdough Toys

111 For extra fun with playdough, give your children special toys to use, such as cookie cutters, small rolling pins, aluminum pans, potato mashers, garlic presses, blunt scissors and plastic eating utensils.

Nonstick Toys

112 Before giving your children cookie cutters or other metal utensils to use with playdough, rub or spray on a little vegetable oil. This will help prevent sticking problems.

Playdough Dispenser

113 Find an empty plastic toothpaste tube. Cut off the bottom and fill the tube with playdough. Let your children squeeze the playdough out through the top of the tube in long strands to create designs on a tabletop.

Making Playdough at Home

114 At the beginning of the school year, have your children take home copies of a playdough recipe. Ask each family to make a batch with their children to send to school (and perhaps a batch to keep at home). The children will enjoy using and sharing the playdough they helped to make.

Playdough Recipes

Easy Playdough

115
1 cup flour
½ cup salt
6 to 7 tablespoons water
1 tablespoon vegetable oil
Drops of food coloring

Mix all ingredients together well. Store in an airtight container in a refrigerator.

Peanut Butter Playdough

116
Mix together equal amounts of peanut butter and powdered milk to make a tasty, edible playdough. Adjust the ingredients as needed if the dough is too soft or too hard.

Brown Playdough

117
In a bowl, mix together 3 cups whole-wheat flour and ½ cup vegetable oil. Add small amounts of water until the mixture is the desired consistency.

Rubber Stamps

Rubber Stamp Collection

118
Purchase a number of rubber stamps in the shapes of pictures and simple words. Your children can use the stamps with commercial ink pads to make greeting cards, wrapping paper, gift stationery, etc.

Office Stamps

119
Rubber stamps don't have to be fancy to be fun to use. Ask businesses to donate old or outdated office stamps such as air-mail stamps.

Unwanted Stamps

120
Office-supply stores are sometimes willing to give away rubber stamps that were made to order but never purchased.

Rubber Stamp Resources

121
Check an office-supply store for the names of rubber stamp companies in your area. Some companies often sell samples inexpensively.

Rejuvenating Rubber Stamps

122 Bring old rubber stamps back to life by scrubbing them with an old toothbrush under hot running water.

Homemade Rubber Stamps

123 Cut simple shapes out of an old rubber inner tube from a car or a bicycle tire. Attach the shapes to wooden blocks with heavy-duty glue to make your own rubber stamps.

Eraser Rubber Stamp

124 Purchase a large, square art gum eraser and use a craft knife to carve a design into one side. Press the carved design on an ink pad, then on paper to make prints.

Letter Stamps

125 When making your own rubber stamps, remember that alphabet letters must be reversed in order to make correct prints.

Scissors

Egg Carton Scissors Holder

126 To store children's scissors neatly, turn a cardboard egg carton upside down and make a hole in the bottom of each egg cup. Then stick the scissors, blade ends down, into the holes.

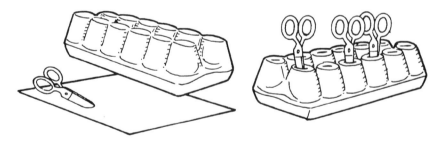

Storing and Toting Scissors

127 A large whipped-topping tub with a lid can be used for storing and toting children's scissors. Simply turn the tub upside down and use a knife to poke holes in the bottom. Insert a pair of scissors, blade end down, in each hole to store. Whenever you need to take the scissors outdoors or on a field trip, just open the tub lid and put the scissors inside.

Sharpening Scissors

128 Dull scissors can be frustrating for children to use. To sharpen dull scissors, snip them through sandpaper a few times. (This is not recommended for expensive shears.)

Other Scissor Sharpeners

129 Try sharpening dull scissors by snipping them through steel wool pads several times. (This is not recommended for expensive shears.)

Holding Scissors

130 When your children are practicing their scissor skills, encourage them to put both their pointer and middle fingers into the scissor's lower hole. This will provide them with more control while they are cutting.

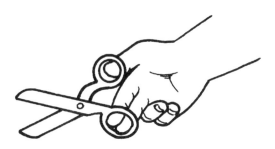

Snip, Snip, Snip

131 For a first cutting experience, try this. Show your children how to hold and manipulate their scissors. Then let them have fun snipping strips of paper into little pieces.

Feeding Hungry Scissors

132 If your children tend to tear through paper while they are cutting, encourage them to "feed the paper slowly to the hungry scissors." This will help them learn how to move the paper toward the blades while holding their scissors steady.

Fancy Paper Chains

133 Help your children make fancy paper chains while they practice their cutting skills. Give each child a piece of paper folded in half lengthwise. Show the child how to make cuts starting at the fold that go almost to the edge of the open side. Then help the child turn the paper around and cut between the first cuts, starting each cut at the open end and going almost to the edge of the fold. Unfold the paper to reveal a beautiful paper chain!

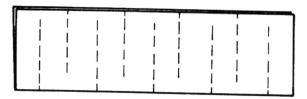

Scissor Safety

134 Sing the following song with your children to reinforce scissor safety.

Sung to: "Row, Row, Row Your Boat"

Walk, walk with your scissors
Always pointed down.
And when you're done put them away—
Don't leave them around.

Janice Bodenstedt

Stickers

Stamplike Stickers

135 Save the stickers that come in the mail from sweepstakes organizers and nonprofit groups. Let your children use the stickers for art projects or as pretend postage stamps.

Homemade Sticker Recipe 1

136 Combine ⅔ cup white glue and ⅓ cup white vinegar. Cover the back side of a piece of paper with the mixture, using a foam paintbrush. When dry, apply a second coat. Allow the paper to dry again. Then turn the paper over and stamp small designs on it. Cut out the stamped designs and you'll have a set of stickers to lick and stick when ever you wish.

Homemade Sticker Recipe 2

137 In a small saucepan, combine 1 package unflavored gelatin, 2 tablespoons fruit juice and a dash of sugar. Heat just until the gelatin is completely dissolved. Use a paintbrush to paint the mixture on the back of paper that you want to use for making stickers. Allow the paper to dry, cut out sticker shapes, then lick and stick.

Wrapping Paper Stickers

138 Find a sheet of giftwrap paper printed with a pattern of small pictures such as toys, animals or flowers. Brush the back of the sheet with one of the home-made sticker mixtures from the recipes above. When the paper dries, cut out the small pictures to make stickers.

Stamped Stickers

139 Check an office-supply store for solid-colored stickers in the shapes of circles and rectangles. Perk up the stickers by using tiny rubber stamps to print designs on them. Allow the ink to dry before peeling the stickers from their backing sheets.

Wrapping Tape Stickers

140 Purchase 1½-inch-wide wrapping tape (the kind you moisten). Cut the tape into pieces. Let your children decorate the tape pieces with crayons or felt-tip markers to make stickers or pretend postage stamps.

Address Label Stickers

141 Give your children plain white address labels. Let them draw designs on the labels with felt-tip markers to make their own stickers.

Sticker Cutouts

142 Select colored or patterned self-stick paper. Cut shapes out of the paper to use as stickers. When you're ready to attach the shapes, just peel off the backing. The stickers can be placed on a sheet of waxed paper before being used.

Peeling Off Stickers

143 Before giving a young child a sheet of commercial stickers, peel off the background, leaving the stickers attached. This allows room for little fingers to peel stickers from the sheet easily.

Storing Stickers

144 Use an accordion-style coupon folder for organizing and storing commercial stickers. The compartments will allow you to file your stickers by subject or season.

Removing Stickers

145 Here's an easy way to remove stickers from wood surfaces. Sponge on white vinegar, allow it to soak in, then scrape off the sticky paper.

Tape

Quick Tape Tip

146 Make tape easily available to your children when they do art activities. Just stick pieces of the tape along the edges of the work table.

Tape Holders

147 If tape is required for art projects, cut it into pieces ahead of time. Then make tape holders for your children by lightly sticking the pieces around the edges of tuna fish cans.

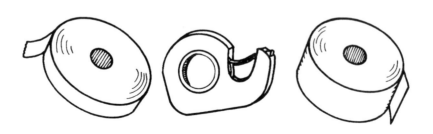

Using Tape Wisely

148 At art time, young children often want to play with tape rather than use it for making things. Solve the problem by giving them separate pieces of tape to play with and hold.

Weaving

Plastic Mesh

149 Look in a hardware store for strips of plastic mesh that are used to keep gutters from clogging. The 6-inch-wide mesh comes in rolls about 8 yards long and can be cut into pieces to use for weaving projects. Be sure to tape around any rough edges first.

Toothbrush Needles

150 Save old toothbrushes that have holes in the ends. Cut off and discard the brush parts, keeping the parts with holes to use as weaving needles. Use sandpaper to round off and smooth the rough ends. You'll find that these needles are easy for little hands to thread and hold.

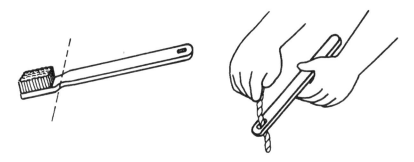

Yarn Needles

151 When your children are weaving with yarn, make "needles" by wrapping the ends of the yarn pieces with tape. Or dip the ends into glue, nail polish or melted candle wax and let them dry.

More Art Tips

Drawing Paper

152 Business offices often save unwanted sheets of computer paper or copy-machine paper for recycling. Even if the paper has writing on it, your children can still use the blank sides for drawing or coloring.

Make-Up Pencils

153 Save old or unwanted make-up pencils, including those used for lining brows, lips and eyes. Your children can use the pencils for art projects. The pencils are greasy, so have the children wear smocks when they color.

Dyeing Pasta

154 To dye ½ cup uncooked pasta, shake the pasta pieces in a reclosable plastic bag with about 10 drops of food coloring and ¼ teaspoon rubbing alcohol. Arrange the dyed pasta pieces on paper towels. The rubbing alcohol produces strong colors and helps the pasta dry quickly without sticking.

Making Confetti

155 Save all your scraps of colored paper, even the smallest pieces. Let your children make confetti by using a hole punch to punch tiny circles out of the scraps. Keep the confetti for decorating art projects.

Spatter Painting

156 Round spatter screens that are placed over frying pans to keep grease off stoves can be used with toothbrushes for spatter painting. Look for the screens in the kitchenware departments of large stores.

Sanding Clay Artwork

157 Keep a supply of inexpensive emery boards to use for sanding art pieces that require smoothing before painting.

Braiding Made Easier

158 Try this when helping your children learn to braid ribbon, fabric or thick yarn pieces. Tie the pieces together at one end. Then put the knot under the clip on a clipboard to hold the materials securely as they work.

Papier-Mache Adhesive

159 When doing papier-mache projects, try using liquid starch instead of wallpaper paste. The starch is easier to use and dries more quickly.

Art Stencils

160 Save the plastic lids from margarine, whipped-topping and cottage-cheese containers. Cut circles, triangles, stars, etc., out of the lids to make stencils for your children to use for art projects.

Art Feathers

161 For art projects that require feathers (such as making chick collages) buy a colored feather duster. It will cost less than buying feathers in a craft store.

Shaker Containers

162 Save seasoning and herb jars with perforated lids. The jars are great for dispensing glitter, sand, salt, etc., and are easy for little hands to hold.

Art Supplies Tote

163 Use a cardboard six-pack carrier to make a tote for holding art supplies. Spray-paint the carrier, if desired, in an area away from children. When dry, fill the compartments with a variety of art materials such as glue, crayons, felt-tip markers and scissors.

Coordination Tips

Dressing Skills

Practice Makes Perfect

164 Start at the beginning of the school year to provide your children with plenty of time to practice dressing skills. When winter approaches and more clothing is required, the children will feel more confident about trying to dress themselves.

Zippering, Buttoning and Snapping

165 From old clothing, cut out strips of fabric that contain large zippers, buttons and matching button holes, and sets of snaps. Place the fabric strips in a box for your children to play with.

Putting on Training Pants

166 Use fabric markers on pairs of white training pants to color the leg openings one color and the waist bands another color. This makes it easier for young children to tell which openings are which when they put the training pants on.

Putting on a Sweater

167 Help a child lay out his or her sweater front side down. Show the child how to go in through the bottom of the sweater and stick his or her head and arms out through the appropriate holes. Soon the child should be able to lay out the sweater and put it on without help.

Buttoning Coats

168 Have your children start at the bottom when buttoning up coats or jackets. They'll be more likely to get all the buttons in the right buttonholes.

Shoes on the Right Feet

169 To help your children put their shoes on the right feet, try this. Mark the inside arches of their shoes with red arrows that point inward when the left and right shoes are in the correct positions.

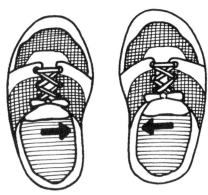

Shoe Lacing Practice

170 Pairs of old shoes with long laces are great for young children to practice lacing and unlacing.

Manipulatives

Locks and Latches

171 Purchase latches and locks at a hardware store. Attach them to a wall or a board and let your children have fun manipulating them.

Twist and Bend

172 For fun manipulatives, give your children different materials to bend and twist with their fingers. For instance, include pipe cleaners, bendable curlers, twist ties and pieces of colored telephone wire.

Nuts and Bolts

173 Large nuts and bolts that fit together make great manipulatives for young children. Look for these nuts and bolts at a hardware store.

Tossing and Catching Toys

Mitten Beanbags

174 Here's a quick way to make beanbags. Just fill old mittens with dried beans and sew the wrists closed with heavy yarn or thread.

Shoulder Pad Beanbag

175 Make a beanbag out of an old shoulder pad. Carefully pull out part of a seam. Put dried beans into the pad until it is the desired weight, then sew the seam back up again.

Beanbag Bonzo

176 For a fun beanbag catcher, paint a clown face on the side of a cardboard carton and cut out a large circle for its mouth. Your children can toss beanbags through the hole to "feed Bonzo."

Sock Ball

177 Here's something you can do with a mismatched sock from your lost-and-found box. Roll it up, fold over the opening, and use it as a ball for tossing and catching games.

Other Tossing Toys

178 Let your children try tossing and catching items such as small sponges, balls of yarn or crumpled newspaper balls.

More Coordination Tips

Preparing Snacks

179 Involve your children in preparing snacks. Activities such as spreading food, grating and stirring help develop small muscle coordination.

Cleaning Chores

180 Let your children help with cleaning chores such as mopping floors, wiping tables, or washing windows. These whole-body movements develop large muscle coordination.

Eye Coordination

181 Try this for developing eye coordination. Hang a plastic-foam ball on a string from the ceiling. Ask your children to follow the movement of the ball with their eyes as you swing it back and forth. Remind them to keep their heads still.

Eye-Hand Coordination

182 Hammering is great for developing eye-hand coordination. Your children can pound nails into wood or golf tees into chunks of plastic foam.

Language Tips

Letter Recognition

Special Letter Containers

183 When introducing a new letter of the alphabet, make a special container to fill with items whose names begin with that letter. For instance, put *H* items in a hat or *J* items in a pair of jeans with the legs tied or stitched shut.

"B" Is for Buttons

184 Your children will have fun learning the alphabet if you let them glue appropriate items on large letter shapes. For instance, give them buttons to glue on *B* shapes, feathers to glue on *F* shapes, or toothpicks to glue on *T* shapes.

Letters and Pictures

185 Turn your walls into a giant "alphabet book." Display the letters of the alphabet around the room. Whenever a child brings in a special picture to share, hang it by the letter that begins its name.

Edible Letters

186 Alphabet cereal pieces and cooked alphabet noodles are fun and tasty aids for teaching letter recognition.

Take-Home Items

187 Reinforce letter recognition skills by giving your children alphabet take-home items such as paper cookie shapes for *C* or paper egg shapes for *E*. Label the items with the appropriate letters.

Letter Day

188 Here's a fun way to review an alphabet letter. Have a Letter Day on which everyone brings in items that have the requested letter printed on them (magazine covers, cereal boxes, T-shirts, toys, etc.). Also, plan games and snacks with names that begin with that letter.

Listening

Being a Good Listener

189 Developing listening skills takes patience and practice. Show your children what it means to be a good listener by giving them your full attention when they are talking to you.

Open Your Ears

190 Help your children become aware of the sounds around them by having them pause throughout the day to "open their ears." What new sounds can they hear and identify?

Do and Tell

191 A good way to help develop listening skills is to explain your actions to your children while you are doing tasks. For instance, when you are straightening up the art area you might say, "I'm putting the crayons in the blue can and the markers in the yellow box."

Pre-Reading and Pre-Writing

Say It in Writing

192 Help your children begin to relate to reading and writing by printing simple sentences on strips of paper to accompany bulletin board displays, science projects, artwork, etc.

Eye-Level Reading

193 To make reading an integral part of your children's world, display written materials, such as posters or story charts, at the children's eye level.

Author! Author!

194 Encourage interest in reading and writing by helping your children write their own books. Provide wallpaper samples to make special book covers, if desired.

My Own Words

195 When young children dictate stories to you, be sure to write down exactly what they say. Hearing their own words read back to them will help them begin to understand the relationship between spoken and written language.

Writing Names

196 Use your children's names to introduce reading and writing skills. Label the children's belongings with their names and encourage them to copy their names on paper.

Tracing Letters

197 Encourage beginning writing skills by laminating alphabet letters for your children to trace over with wax crayons or grease pencils.

Greeting Card Messages

198 Provide opportunities for your children to make and send group greeting cards. As they dictate thank-you or get-well messages for you to write down, they'll be developing pre-reading and pre-writing skills.

Typewriter Fun

199 Let your children play with an old typewriter or computer keyboard. Although they won't be able to type, they'll begin to learn that the letters on the keys can be used to make words.

Relaxed Environment

200 A relaxed environment is best for encouraging beginning writing. Allow experimentation and don't force drill. Above all, be sure to give your children lots of praise.

Puppets

Paper Towel Puppets

201 Thick, spongy paper towels can be cut and sewn into mitten shapes for hand puppets. Slip cardboard inside the shapes before decorating them with felt-tip markers. That way, the ink won't soak through to the back of the puppet.

Finger Puppet Faces

202 When drawing faces on your children's fingers to make puppets, try using grease pencils instead of felt-tip markers. The pencils come in a variety of colors, and the marks are easy to wash off.

Create-A-Face Puppet

203 Cut a circle out of posterboard for a puppet face and cover it with clear self-stick paper. Glue on yarn hair, if desired, and attach the face to a craft stick. Let your children use wax crayons to draw facial features on the puppet. When they want to change the puppet's face, they can wipe off the crayon marks with a facial tissue and draw on new features.

Kangaroo Puppet

204 Use a kangaroo puppet when teaching numbers or the letters of the alphabet. Have the puppet hop from letter to letter or numeral to numeral as you say the letters or numbers aloud.

Puppet Mascot

205 Adopt an attractive puppet for a class mascot. Your new friend can help greet the children, serve as a listening ear for a shy child, and announce transition times.

Puppet Theater

206 Here's an inexpensive way to make a puppet theater. Find a refrigerator carton and remove the back. Then cut a window in the front at an appropriate height. Your children can stand inside the carton to put on puppet shows.

Story Motivators

Postcard Storytelling

207 Save picture postcards you receive in the mail and place them in a box. At circle time, let your children take turns drawing the postcards out of the box to use as props for making up a story.

Picture File

208 Keep a file of interesting or unusual pictures on hand. Select one at language time and encourage your children to make up a story about it.

Story Time

Story Chair

209 Brighten an old chair with a new coat of paint and use it as your special story chair. Whenever your children see you sitting in it, they will know that it's time to gather around for story time.

Reading Out Loud

210 Before you read a book to your children, go through it once or twice by yourself. Being familiar with the story will allow you to relax and enjoy sharing the book with your group.

Reading Time

211 Consider your children's attention span when choosing books for story time. As a rule of thumb, books for young children should take from 5 to 10 minutes to read aloud.

Story Props

212 Your children will find story time even more fun if you use props. For instance, when telling the story of the three bears, some props might be three sizes of teddy bears, bowls and chairs.

Audience Size

213 If you work with a large group, try dividing your children into smaller groups for story time. It's important for young children to be able to see the pictures clearly when you are reading a book to them.

Telling Stories Together

214 At story time, let your children help you tell familiar tales. This will encourage them to become active participants in the reading process.

Guest Readers

215 Set aside one day each week for a guest reader to come in for story time. People who enjoy doing this include parents, grandparents, older students and other teachers. Offer assistance in selecting books to those who want it.

Book Care

216 Use story time to discuss how to take care of books. Be aware that your children will model the way you feel about books and how you handle them.

Library Visit

217 To spruce up your reading corner, plan a trip to your local library to check out books. Let your children help with the selection.

Inexpensive Bookmarks

218 Wallpaper samples cut into 2-inch-wide strips make pretty bookmarks. You might want to give one to each of your children.

Decorated Bookmarks

219 Cut corners off old envelopes to slip over the corners of book pages for bookmarks. Your children can decorate the bookmarks and place them in a basket. Choose one at story time as needed.

Learning Game Tips

Blindfold Alternatives

Stocking Cap Blindfold

220 If you have a child who dislikes being blindfolded for games, let the child wear a stocking cap and pull it down over his or her eyes. Wearing the cap will help the child feel more in control.

Dark Glasses

221 Instead of using a blindfold for games, try this. Let your children wear a small pair of sunglasses with paper circles taped or glued over the lenses.

Hide Your Eyes

222 If your children don't like being blindfolded for games, simply have them cover their eyes with their hands or close their eyes tightly. Remind them, no peeking!

Left-Right Discrimination

Puppet Fun

223 To help your children learn to distinguish their right hands from their left, use a puppet to shake hands with them at the beginning of each day. Whenever necessary, remind the children that their right hands are the ones they use when they shake hands with the puppet.

Trace and Match

224 Trace around each child's right hand and left hand on a piece of construction paper. Label the shapes "Left" and "Right," cover them with clear self-stick paper, and cut them out. Fasten each child's shapes together with a piece of yarn. Then let the children practice matching their left and right hands with the paper cutouts.

"L" Is for Left

225 Here's an easy way for your children to remember which hand is their left one. Have them hold up their hands, palms out, with their fingers together and their thumbs outstretched. The forefinger and thumb of their left hand will form an *L* shape.

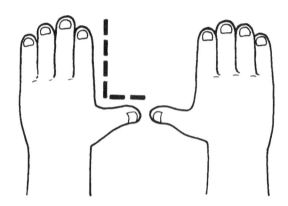

Matching Games

Paint Sample Strips

226 Use paint sample strips from a paint store to make color matching games.

Plastic Clothespins

227 Colored plastic clothespins are great to use for color matching games. Your children can clip the clothespins to matching colored squares of paper or fabric.

Colored Barrettes

228 Plastic hair barrettes come in a variety of colors. Purchase them at drugstores or variety stores to use for color matching games.

Colorful Note Cards

229 Ask family members and friends to donate pairs of leftover note cards that have pictures on the fronts. The pictures are perfect for making matching games.

Leaf Rubbings

230 For a nature matching game, make two rubbings each of several different leaves and attach them to posterboard squares.

Matching Game Pictures

231 Cut pairs of pictures from patterned wrapping paper or wallpaper. Glue the pictures on posterboard squares to make cards for matching games.

Number Games

Math Counters

232 For math counters, use everyday items such as buttons, dried beans, clothespins, cotton swabs, paper clips, cotton balls or drinking straws.

Edible Math Counters

233 Small food items, such as cereal pieces, raisins, pretzels and carrot sticks, make tasty math counters.

Textured Number Cards

234 Print numerals on squares of heavy cardboard. Then glue on matching numbers of small buttons, sandpaper circles or flocked stickers for the children to touch and count.

Handy Number Cards

235 Trace around a child's hands and cut five pairs of the shapes from construction paper. Number the right-hand shapes from 1 to 5 and draw a matching number of dots on each left-hand shape. Cover the shapes with clear self-stick paper. Then give them to the child to use as a personal set of number-matching cards.

Counting Books

236 Learning numbers will be fun for your children when they make their own counting books. Provide them with blank books made from construction paper that contain several pages each. Number the pages and let the children add matching numbers of dots, stickers, thumbprints, etc.

Related Learning

237 Relate number learning to other curriculum areas. For instance, combine learning the number 8 with a unit on spiders, or discuss shamrocks when teaching the number 3.

Telling Time

238 For young children who are beginning to learn how to tell time, make a cardboard clock that has just an hour hand. A minute hand can be added later when the children become more skilled at telling time.

Counting Bank

239 Find an empty disposable-wipe container. Cut a slit in the lid to make a bank for your children to use with play money.

Playing Cards

240 Use a deck of ordinary playing cards for number-matching games.

Calendar Numerals

241 Cut numerals out of old calendars. They are great for making number-matching game cards or faces on paper-plate clocks.

Puzzles

Board-Book Page Puzzles

242 If you have a children's board book that contains some damaged pages, don't throw the book away. Instead, cut all the pages out of the book and discard the ruined ones. Then cut each remaining page into strips or free-form pieces to make a puzzle. (Do the cutting with a pair of very strong scissors, a heavy-duty paper cutter or a scroll saw.) Store the pieces of each puzzle in a reclosable plastic bag.

How Many Pieces?

243 You might wish to follow these general guidelines when making jigsaw puzzles. For toddlers, cut each puzzle into 3 or 4 pieces. For 3-year-olds, cut each puzzle into 6 to 10 pieces, and for 4- and 5-year-olds, cut each puzzle into 8 to 12 pieces.

Homemade Picture Puzzles

244 To make your own puzzles, cut pictures from magazines, mount them on plain paper, then cover them on both sides with clear self-stick paper. Cut each picture into the desired number of puzzle pieces.

Seasonal Puzzles

245 Save pictures from old calendars to make seasonal puzzles. Follow the directions above for making picture puzzles.

Food Box Puzzles

246 Cut the fronts off cookie boxes, cereal boxes, etc. Cover each box front with clear self-stick paper and cut it into puzzle pieces.

Preventing Puzzle Mix-Ups 1

247 To keep the pieces of a puzzle from getting mixed up with those of other puzzles, write the name of the puzzle on the back of each piece.

Preventing Puzzle Mix-Ups 2

248 Draw an identical colored dot on the back of each piece in a puzzle. You'll be able to tell at a glance which pieces belong together.

Puzzling Challenges

249 Do your children have commercial puzzles that are no longer challenging? Have them try putting the pieces together with the frames turned sideways or upside down. Or let the children assemble the pieces on a tabletop or the floor without the frames.

Stray Puzzle Pieces

250 Here's a great way to make use of stray puzzle pieces that always seem to accumulate. Place all the pieces on a large sheet of white paper. Trace around each puzzle piece, copy the designs, and fill in the colors with felt-tip markers. Then laminate the paper and put the puzzle pieces in a reclosable plastic bag. Your children can use the laminated paper as a game board and place the puzzle pieces on the matching shapes.

Sorting Games

Sorting Napkin Rings

251 Set out a baby bottle drying rack and several kinds of napkin rings. Your children can sort the rings by placing each kind on a different peg of the rack.

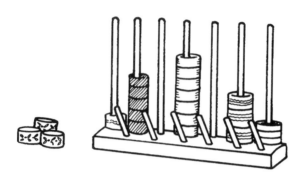

Bread Closers

252 Ask parents to save the small plastic squares that are used to keep bread packages closed. Let your children sort them by color.

Caps and Lids

253 Save lids and caps from several kinds of containers. Keep them in a box for your children to sort by shape, color, size, etc.

Sorting Trays

254 Egg cartons make perfect trays for sorting small items such as buttons, dried beans, beads and pasta shapes.

Cleanup Time Sorting

255 Whenever your children are putting away their toys, turn the task into a sorting game. Or let them help you sort collage materials, beads, math counters, etc., into separate containers when you are straightening up your work area.

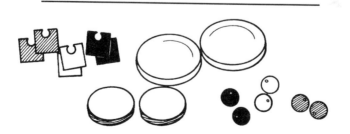

More Learning Game Tips

Starting the Week Right

256 Begin each Monday in a fun way by bringing in a giftwrapped toy or other surprise. Have your children try to guess what it is. Let the child who first guesses correctly open the package for the group.

Calendar Fun

257 Make a calendar for a week or a month. In each day's space, write a special activity for your children. Try some of these: "Find something blue. Make a wish. Help make hot chocolate." Checking the calendar each morning will become a special event!

Shoe Boxes

258 Empty shoe boxes are great for making learning games or storing game parts. Check shoe stores to see if they will donate boxes.

Write On, Wipe Off

259 Use plastic sheet protectors (available at office-supply stores) to cover small game boards. Provide washable felt-tip markers. Your children can use the write-on, wipe-off boards over and over again to play games.

Learning With Boxes

260 A collection of empty boxes is perfect for teaching concepts such as counting, matching, sorting (by size, color, construction, etc.), opposites (open-closed, light-heavy, etc.), size relationships (big, bigger, biggest, etc.), and space relationships (inside, next to, through, etc.).

Introducing New Items

261 Try this for stimulating interest when introducing a new game, book, toy, etc. Put the special item into a bag and let your children ask questions about it that you can answer with a yes or no. After a designated number of questions have been asked, the children can whisper what they think is inside the bag before you reveal its contents.

Learning Lunch Box

262 Put small items, such as crayons, a note pad, a puzzle, and a set of counting cards, into a decorated lunch box. Give the lunch box to a child to play with as a special treat during free time. Check the "learning lunch box" often and change or add items as needed.

Music Tips

Classical Music

Watch Me Play

263 To introduce a musical instrument that is played in an orchestra, bring in an example of the instrument or display a picture of it. Then put on a recording of orchestra music and let your children pretend to play along on the selected instrument.

Conductor

264 Help your children develop a feel for classical music by letting them "conduct" with cardboard tube batons while listening to a recording.

Instrument Demonstration

265 Classical music will come alive for your children if you invite adults to visit your group and demonstrate various instruments.

Classical Music Resources

Check the Library

266 Visit your local library to find classical music recordings that can be checked out. Ask the librarian for specific pieces or suggestions for appropriate selections.

Violin Music

267 To introduce your children to violin music, try playing recordings of violin concertos by Mozart, Brahms or Mendelssohn.

Upbeat Classical Music

268 For upbeat classical selections, play a recording of Tchaikovsky's *Nutcracker Suite* or Mozart's *Eine Kleine Nacht Musick*, first movement.

Mellow Classical Music

269 If you wish to introduce quieter classical selections, try playing recordings of Pachelbel's *Canon* or the second movement of Mozart's *Eine Kleine Nacht Musick*.

Musical Activities

Music and Art

270 Let your children paint as they listen to music. Cut the dry paintings into giant musical notes and mount them on a wall or a bulletin board with the caption "Music in the Air."

Musical Hugs

271 Instead of Musical Chairs, play Musical Hugs. Clear a large space in your room for the children to move about in while listening to music. Whenever the music stops, have everyone hug someone nearby. If several children are close together, they can have a group hug.

Musical Classics

272 Before telling your children the story of a musical classic, such as Tchaikovsky's *Peter and the Wolf*, follow the Suzuki method of letting them listen to the piece as background music for several weeks. When you tell the story, the children already will have learned to distinguish the various melodies and to anticipate what comes next. Follow up with another few weeks of listening, and your children will never forget the music they learned.

Musical Walks

273 Help your children become more aware of the music in their environment. Take them on special walks to listen for musical sounds such as bells, bird songs, or melodies played by street musicians.

Music Store Visit

274 Visiting a music store is a great way to introduce young children to both classical and pop instruments. Arrange for someone to demonstrate how the instruments are played, if possible.

Playing Instruments

Music Boxes

275 To foster an interest in music, give very young children music-box toys that they can play by turning a crank.

Play Along

276 To develop auditory discrimination, tape-record a piece of music, occasionally changing the volume from loud to soft. Then have your children accompany the music with rhythm instruments and adjust their playing whenever they hear a volume change on the tape.

Shoulder Pad Shaker

277 Use an old shoulder pad to make a shaker for music activities. Carefully take out part of a seam. Push a jingle bell through the opening and into the padding. Then sew the seam back up again.

Musical Instrument Box

278 Set out a box of musical instruments for your children to experiment with during free time. Garage sales are great places to find inexpensive tambourines, drums, kazoos, xylophones and guitars.

Songs

Ask a Friend

279 If you don't play a musical instrument, ask a friend who plays the piano or guitar to record the tunes of your children's favorite songs on tape.

Favorite Song List

280 Keep on hand a list of the songs you have taught your children. Most children enjoy singing old favorites, and it's easy to forget which songs they know. The list will also be useful if you ever need a substitute teacher.

Song Box

281 Here's a way to guarantee fair turns when choosing songs to sing. In a box, place slips of paper on which you have written the titles of favorite songs. Then let your children take turns selecting song titles from the box.

Hula Hoop Props

282 When singing the songs on children's records that are called "circle games," use Hula Hoops as props.

Where's That Tune?

283 Use a permanent felt-tip marker to indicate the beginning of a favorite song on the clear-plastic viewing window of an audio cassette tape. You will no longer need to hunt and wait to find the exact spot you want.

The Wheels on the Bus

284 "The Wheels on the Bus" is always fun to sing, but sometimes the bouncing up and down can get out of hand. To discourage this and to encourage the use of seatbelts, have your children pretend to buckle up before they begin singing. No longer will little bodies be bouncing out of chairs!

For Fun

285 Just for fun, try singing a familiar song with your children in different ways—fast then slow, loud then soft, with high voices then low voices. Can your children come up with other ways to sing?

Sing, Sing, Sing

286 Sing songs with your children whenever you go on a walk or a field trip. It's a fun way to relieve restlessness and keep everyone together.

Year-Round Caroling

287 Caroling need not be just for holiday time. Take your children to nursing homes, to children's hospitals or just around the neighborhood to sing favorite songs any time of the year.

Play and Learning Center Tips

Block Center

Block Building Zone

288 Use a large area rug to define the building zone in your block center.

No-Building Zone

289 Use electrical tape on the floor to mark off a no-building area in your block center so that the children can walk through without knocking over works in progress. Add diagonal strips of yellow tape for emphasis, if desired.

Block Center Extenders

290 To extend block play, add items to your block center, such as toy cars, animals and people. To encourage different kinds of block building, include cardboard traffic and business signs.

Math Fun

291 Have blocks that are multiples of one another in size in your block center. Your children will discover through play that two blocks of one size are equal to one block of another size, and so on.

Learning Shapes

292 To reinforce learning of shapes—especially three-dimensional shapes—include square blocks, rectangular blocks, triangular blocks, etc., in your block center.

Juice Box Blocks

293 Save empty juice boxes, rinse and dry them well, and cover them with colorful self-stick paper for a new set of blocks.

Block Cleanup

294 Attach traced shapes of your blocks to the shelves in your block center. At cleanup time, your children can put the blocks on the proper shelves by matching them to the traced shapes.

Carpentry Center

Carpentry Tools

295 For your carpentry center, purchase real tools in small sizes from a hardware store. Suggested tools include claw and ball-peen hammers, coping and hand saws, Phillips and ordinary screwdrivers, a hand drill, rasps, nails with large heads, pliers, C-clamps, a ruler, a T-square, wood glue and safety goggles.

Tool Storage

296 Try this idea for storing your carpentry tools. Trace each tool shape on a piece of pegboard. Add appropriate hooks and label each tracing. Then hang the pegboard on a wall where your children can easily put the tools away after using them.

Carpentry Workbench

297 For a workbench in your carpentry center, try using a wooden cable spool, a sturdy wooden box or an old table cut down to size.

Scrap Wood Sources

298 Look around for free scrap wood to use in your carpentry center. Local supermarkets may have wooden produce boxes, lumber yards often have scrap piles of free wood, and carpenters or neighbors who are remodeling often have leftover wood scraps.

Carpentry Safety Tips

299 Keep your carpentry center safe by having your children observe these tips.

- Wear safety goggles at all times.
- Use C-clamps to hold boards for hammering or sawing.
- Keep tools in the carpentry area only.
- Put carpentry tools away properly after each use.
- Have adult supervision in the carpentry area at all times.

Dramatic Play Center

Bangle Bracelets

300 Let your children use canning jar rings as golden bangle bracelets for dramatic play.

Dress-Up Clothes Sachet

301 Place a handful of cedar chips (available at pet stores or farmers' co-ops as bedding material) in a square of nylon netting. Bring the corners of the netting together and tie securely with a piece of string. Place this cedar-chip sachet in your box of dress-up clothes to protect them from moths or mildew.

Coupon Book Fun

302 Place outdated supper club or entertainment coupon books in your dramatic play center. Your children can tear out the coupons and use them as play money for pretend activities such as eating at a restaurant, going to the theater, or taking an airplane ride.

Storybook Play

303 Use dramatic play to make reading come alive. In your dramatic play center, include clothing or costumes that your children can use to dress up as their favorite storybook characters.

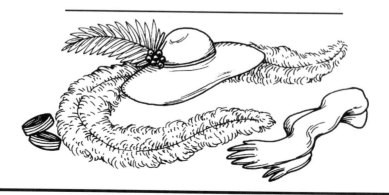

General Organization

Color Codes

304 Use a different color to mark off and decorate each of the areas in your room. If desired, coordinate the colors with the mood desired in each area. For instance, use red for the art area, green for the quiet area, and so on. Color coding in this way will help your children to easily recognize the separate areas.

Instant Learning Centers

305 Make an instant learning center in your room by placing a blanket, a sheet or a Hula Hoop on the floor to define a work space. Or mark off an area on the floor with strips of masking tape.

Learning Center Name Tags

306 To regulate the number of children who can work at one time in a learning center, try this. Provide hooks in each center. (The number of hooks should match the maximum number of children appropriate at each center.) Cut seasonal shapes from stiff paper. Write each child's name on a shape and punch holes in the tops. Your children can hang their shapes on the hooks for each center while they are working, then take them down when they leave. Whenever there is an empty hook, a child can enter a center, if he or she wishes.

Jar Lid Name Tags

307 Collect wide-mouth canning jar lids that have one white side. Use a permanent felt-tip marker to write each child's name on a separate lid. Make slots available at each learning center where your children can insert their name tags. When all the slots at a center are full, a child must look for another center to work in.

Housekeeping Center

Housekeeping Props

308 Instead of using regular product containers as props for your housekeeping center, provide single-serving cereal boxes, travel-size shampoo bottles, sample-size hand lotion bottles, etc. The smaller containers are more practical because they take up less space.

Pretend Meals

309 Make inexpensive props for your housekeeping center by gluing to paper plates pictures of foods that illustrate well-balanced breakfasts, lunches and dinners. Cover the plates with clear self-stick paper to make them last longer.

Doll Clothes

310 Collect old baby clothes to place in your housekeeping center. Your children can use them for dressing dolls or stuffed animals.

Library Center

Cut Down on Noise

311 A rug placed on the floor in your library center will help muffle noise.

Book Display

312 Make it easy for your children to select books to read in your library center. Place the books on low shelves with their covers facing out.

Hanging Book Holder

313 Hang up a diaper stacker to use as a mini-book holder or a bookshelf. Stack books one on top of the other inside it.

Listening Center

Organizing Tapes and Books

314 Organize the tapes and books in your listening center by placing each set in a gallon-size reclosable plastic bag. Label the parts of each set—the bag, tape and book (or books)—with matching stickers so that your children can identify them easily.

Homemade Tape Tip

315 When making tape recordings of storybooks for your listening corner, give the signal for turning a page as, "It's time to turn the page now," or "Please turn the page." This kind of signal works better for young children than ringing a bell.

Using a Tape Recorder

316 To help your children remember how to operate the tape recorder in your listening center, try this. Put red tape on the stop button, yellow tape on the rewind button, and green tape on the play button.

Tape Container

317 Use a plastic disposable-wipe container as a holder for audiotapes.

Tape Tote

318 For storing and toting audiotapes, use a child-size plastic lunch box.

Post Office Center

Post Office Props

319 For fun post office props, use junk mail for letters, the fronts of greeting cards for picture postcards, and stamplike stickers for postage stamps.

Cancellation Stamp

320 Let your children use a small sink plug with a commercial ink pad to "cancel" letters in your post office center.

Reusing Envelopes

321 If you want to use junk-mail envelopes to mail letters at a real post office, be sure to black out the bar codes as well as any writing on the envelopes. The bar codes contain information that may send your letters to unwanted destinations.

More Play and Learning Center Tips

Grocery Store Center

322 Set up a grocery store in your room for dramatic play. Place a tall appliance box on its side for a counter. Make shelves from smaller boxes and stock them with a wide assortment of empty food boxes for groceries.

Looking Center

323 Young children love playing with shiny objects that reflect a distorted image. Set up a looking corner and stock it with reflectors such as aluminum foil, foil wallpaper, shiny hubcaps, and an old chrome coffeepot or toaster.

Science Tips

Birds

Materials for Nests

324 At nesting time, put a box containing dryer lint and pieces of string outdoors. Look for birds to take the materials for building their nests.

Easy Bird Feeder

325 Save the shell from half a grapefruit to make a bird feeder. Punch four holes near the top of the shell and use string to hang it from a tree branch. Fill your feeder with seeds or nuts.

Bird Feeding Commitment

326 If you start feeding the birds in your yard at winter time, be sure to continue doing so until spring arrives. The birds will come to depend on the food you give them to survive during the cold season.

Indoor Gardens

Fast-Sprouting Seeds

327 If you want quick results for seed-sprouting projects, use alfalfa seeds (available in health food stores or large supermarkets).

Carrot Top Garden

328 Save the orange tops that you cut off raw carrots when preparing them for eating. Stand the carrot tops in a shallow tray. Place the tray in a sunny spot, keep it filled with water, and watch for roots and lacy greenery to appear.

Citrus Orchard

329 On a sunny windowsill, start your own "citrus orchard" by planting seeds from an orange, a lemon or a grapefruit in a pot of peat moss. Plant the seeds about ½ inch deep and add water regularly to keep the soil moist.

Citrus Seed Planting Tip

330 Make sure you plant citrus seeds as soon as you remove them from the fruit. If you let the seeds dry, they may not sprout.

Sweet Potato Plant

331 One of the easiest and most satisfactory indoor plants to grow is a sweet potato plant. Simply stick toothpicks around the middle of a sweet potato and balance it on the rim of a jar filled with water. Add water as needed to keep the jar full and watch for roots and green vines to appear.

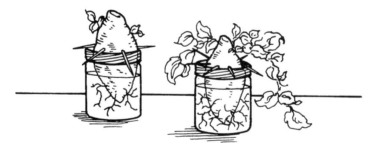

Bottle Cap Planters

332 Save the measuring caps from large bottles of liquid laundry detergent. After rinsing them out thoroughly, give the caps to your children to fill with soil and use as individual planters.

Funny Feet Planters

333 Your children will love this idea! Have them save their old tennis shoes to use as planters. Let them fill the shoes with soil and add seeds or small plants. Place the planters on a tray to catch spills when watering.

Natural Dyes

Boiled Dyes

334 Make natural dyes by boiling the following ingredients in water: red onion skins for red; beets for red violet; cranberries for pink; yellow onion skins for yellow; blackberries for blue; spinach leaves for green; coffee grounds for brown.

No-Cook Dyes

335 For natural dyes that do not require boiling, try experimenting with juices such as grape juice, canned blueberry juice or canned beet juice. (Reserve the fruits or vegetables for other uses.)

Outdoor Gardens

Arbor Day

336 To find out about fun Arbor Day activities and how to order inexpensive tree seedlings, write to National Arbor Day Foundation, 211 N. 12th St., Lincoln, NE 68508.

Good Earth Bug Control

337 To get rid of pesky bugs in your garden, fill spray bottles with a mild solution of 1 part liquid dish-washing detergent to 10 parts water. Let your children spray bug-infested plants with this mixture that will not harm plants or the environment.

Good Earth Slug Control

338 To catch slugs in your garden, turn a grapefruit shell upside down in the dirt. The slugs will collect on the inside and outside of the grapefruit shell. Throw away the shell with the slugs on it as often as needed and replace it with a new one.

Gardening Information

339 Check your local county extension office for free literature about gardening without pesticides.

More Science Tips

Sniffing Jars

340 Use plastic seasoning jars with perforated caps to make containers for sniffing different substances. Glue small circles cut from an old nylon stocking on the undersides of the caps to keep the contents from spilling out.

Magnets Without the Mess

341 Here's a way to avoid spilled metal objects when your children are playing with magnets. Sort small objects (metal paper clips, screws, washers, nuts, etc.) into the compartments of a plastic ice-cube tray. Securely tape or glue a thin, stiff sheet of clear plastic over the top of the tray to make a cover. Let your children move a magnet over the plastic cover and observe what happens.

Transporting an Insect

342 Whenever you need to move an insect from one place to another, try this. Place a glass jar or a see-through plastic tub over the insect. Slip a thin piece of stiff cardboard underneath the mouth of the jar. Then lift the jar while holding the cardboard securely in place and carry the insect to the desired spot.

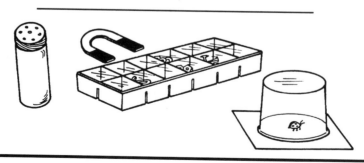

ROOM TIPS

Artwork Tips

Displays

Creative Art Displays

343 Display your children's artwork in unusual or different places. For instance, mount large paintings flat on a ceiling, display translucent artwork in a window, attach pictures to pieces of furniture, or hang murals around the sides of tables.

High-Wire Display

344 String a wire near the ceiling from one corner of your room to another. Clip spring-type clothespins to the wire to use for drying and displaying your children's artwork.

Art Kiosk

345 Stand a large appliance box in a corner of your room. Cover the top and sides of the box with your children's artwork to create a colorful kiosk.

Outdoor Art Show

346 Have an outdoor art show on a sunny day. In addition to displaying your children's work on outside walls, tables and portable easels, include some of these ideas: pictures drawn with colored chalk on a sidewalk; colorful yarn woven through a fence; sculptures created with giant discards; pictures hung from a clothesline with clothespins.

Corner Art Gallery

347 Create an art gallery in a corner of your room. Collect inexpensive picture frames at flea markets and garage sales. Place your children's artwork in the frames, using mats made from construction paper. Hang the pictures at the children's eye level and rotate the art frequently.

About the Artist

348 Spotlight a child's painting or drawing by mounting it at the top of a large piece of posterboard. Below the artwork, attach the child's photo and a typed or hand-printed description that includes the child's name, age, where he or she lives, and two or three of the child's favorite activities. Display the posterboard in a special place in your room.

Picture This

349 Display a child's artwork on a special bulletin board, wall or door. When the display area is full, take a photo of the child with his or her works of art. Place the photo in an album or frame. Then take down the display and start a new one.

Art in the Round

350 Make a three-dimensional art display by trimming a piece of your children's artwork to fit around an empty coffee can. Attach the art with tape or glue.

Box Displays

351 Wrap empty cereal boxes with plain newsprint. Mount children's artwork on the front and back sides of the boxes to make two-sided displays. Set the boxes on tables for easy viewing.

3-D Mounting

352 Cut a flat piece of plastic foam to the size and shape of a child's picture. Glue the picture to the foam piece, then display it on a wall for a three-dimensional effect.

Frames

Wallpaper Frames

353 Cut holes or squares in the centers of wallpaper samples to make frames for your children's artwork. Glue a frame over each child's picture. For a fancy touch, trim the outside edges of the frames with pinking shears.

More Framing Materials

354 For your children's artwork, cut frames out of wrapping paper, stiff fabric, cardboard or corrugated paper.

Poster Frames

355 Plastic poster frames (available at variety stores) are great for displaying children's art. The sides of the frames slide off, making it easy to change displays often.

Craft Stick Frames

356 Make frames for small pictures by gluing craft sticks together in square shapes. The frames can be decorated by your children, if desired.

Shape Frames

357 Cut large seasonal shapes, such as apples, hearts, shamrocks or eggs, from construction paper or posterboard. Attach your children's artwork to the shapes and hang them around your room.

Pretty Picture Frames

358 Cut the tops off decorative facial tissue boxes to use as picture frames. Cover the backs of the box tops with paper, turn them over, and let your children draw or paint inside the frames.

Rickrack Frames

359 Let your children make frames for their own pictures. Have them glue borders of rickrack, ribbon or yarn around the edges of their papers before they begin to draw or paint.

Stick-On Frames

360 Your children can frame their own pictures by pressing on borders of colored plastic tape, patterned self-stick paper, star stickers or self-stick dots.

Hanging Up Artwork

Clip and Hang

361 Tie a spring-type clothespin to one end of a piece of yarn. Hang the yarn from the ceiling so that the clip end of the clothespin is facing down. Write a child's name on a piece of construction paper and tape it to the yarn. Put two pieces of the child's artwork back to back and hang them from the clothespin.

Toothpaste Trick

362 Instead of using tape to hang paper shapes on a wall, try sticking them on with dabs of nongel white toothpaste. The shapes will look nice, and the toothpaste can be washed off the wall when you change decorations.

No More Rips

363 Before using masking tape to hang a poster, apply rubber cement to the areas on the poster where you will be placing the tape. Allow the adhesive to dry before sticking on the tape and hanging the poster. When you take the poster down, the tape will peel off easily without causing rips or tears.

Tape and Hang

364 When your children are making pictures that you want to display on a wall, attach the corners of their papers to a tabletop with masking tape. The tape will keep the papers from sliding. When the children have finished, you can peel the ends of the tape from the table and use them to retape the pictures to the wall.

Paper Clip Hooks

365 Paper clips can be used to make hooks for constructing mobiles and hanging tree decorations or paper shapes. Just unbend the clips to make *S* shapes.

Pipe Cleaner Hangers

366 Twist pipe cleaners into *S* shapes or closed loops and use them for hanging lightweight items.

Preserving Artwork

It's in the Bag

367 Preserve each child's paintings and drawings by placing them in a separate reclosable plastic bag. Keep all your children's bags in a file cabinet or a storage box.

Dry Mounting Pictures

368 Preserve your children's crayon drawings by dry mounting. Place dry-mounting tissue over a picture. Trim the tissue so that it covers the artwork exactly. Cut a piece of posterboard to the desired size. Place the tissue, then the artwork, on top of the posterboard. Put all three pieces inside a dry-mounting press that has been heated to 300°F and heat for 60 seconds. When you take the dry-mounted picture out of the press, lay it flat and cover it with a heavy book to keep it from curling. (Dry-mounting equipment may be available at a local library, school district or parks and recreation department.)

Laminating Artwork

369 Laminating is an easy way to preserve your children's artwork. First, mount a picture as desired. Wrap laminating film around the entire piece of artwork and heat it in a 300°F press for 60 seconds. Trim off excess film after you remove the picture from the press. Cool with a heavy book placed on top to prevent curling. (Check your local library, school district or parks and recreation department to see if laminating equipment is available.)

Preserving Chalk Drawings

370 Children love to color with chalk, but their pictures can be ruined if the chalk smears. Preserve your children's creations by coating them lightly with hairspray. (Use hairspray in an area away from children.)

Punch and Store

371 Preserve each child's artwork by punching holes along one side of each piece and storing it in a personal three-ring binder.

Using Artwork

Colorful Wrapping Paper

372 After your children's artwork has been displayed, let the children use their pictures as wrapping paper for gifts, if they wish.

Stationery Art

373 Turn small pieces of artwork into stationery or note cards. Glue the pictures to folded pieces of construction paper or typing paper.

Duplicated Artwork

374 Use a copy machine to duplicate your children's black-and-white artwork. Cut and fold the copies to make note cards. Let the children color their cards with felt-tip markers.

Banners

375 Turn long, narrow pieces of children's art into banners by attaching them to dowels and tying on yarn hangers.

Patchwork Quilt

376 Create a patchwork quilt with your children's original art. Have the children draw pictures on pieces of white paper with fabric transfer crayons (available at fabric and craft stores). Follow the directions on the crayon box to transfer each design to a piece of cloth. Stitch the fabric pieces together to make a one-of-a-kind quilt.

Cleaning Tips

Cleaning Furniture and Fixtures

Spray-On Cleaner

377 When sanitizing school furniture and fixtures with bleach and water, pour the mixture into an empty window-cleaner spray bottle that has been thoroughly washed and dried. The spray bottle is easy to use and will help prevent "dishpan hands."

Cleaning Highchairs

378 Here's a quick and easy way to clean a highchair. Just place it under a running shower for a few minutes, then give it a good scrubbing. Or clean the chair outside with a garden hose.

Cleaning Playpens

379 Playpens are best cleaned outdoors. Put on rubber gloves, cover them with old white socks, and dip your hands in and out of your wash bucket while you scrub the sides of a mesh playpen. Rinse off suds with a garden hose.

Solving a Sticky Problem

380 After serving a sticky snack, let your children blow bubbles at the cleared-off table. The soapy bubble mix will help make cleaning the tabletop—as well as the children's hands and faces—much easier.

Color It Clean

381 Let your children use colorful soap crayons to draw on the sides and bottom of a dry sink. When they have finished, give them a wet sponge to wash away the colors and clean the sink at the same time.

Keeping Tables Clean

382 An easy and inexpensive way to keep your children's tables clean during art time or snack time is to cover the tables with old fitted bed sheets. The sheets will not slip off the tables and can be washed as needed.

Cleaning Stuffed Toys

No Harsh Cleaners

383 When cleaning stuffed toys, do not use foam carpet cleansers or other harsh cleaners. Young children often put stuffed toys into their mouths.

Washing Stuffed Animals

384 For stuffed animals that have become dingy, try this cleaning method. Put the washable toys into a pillowcase and tie the end closed. Machine wash on a gentle cycle, using cold water and a mild laundry detergent. Do not bleach. Keep the stuffed animals in the pillowcase and tumble dry on a low-heat setting, along with one or two old towels.

Cornmeal Rub

385 Stuffed toys that cannot be laundered need special cleaning. Try rubbing them (or shaking them in a bag) with cornmeal. Leave the cornmeal on the toys for awhile before brushing it off.

Baking Soda Sprinkle

386 When it's time to clean your children's stuffed animals, sprinkle them with baking soda. Then give them a good brushing with a dry brush.

Removing Print

Rubbing It Off

387 Use rubbing alcohol to remove print from plastic egg cartons and margarine tub lids.

Remove Print Fast

388 Nail polish remover quickly removes print from plastic containers such as egg cartons, yogurt cups and whipped-topping tubs. (Work in an area away from children when using nail polish remover.)

Removing Stains

Crayon Marks on Walls

389 Make a paste of baking soda and water. Using a damp sponge, gently rub the paste on walls to remove crayon marks.

Crayon Marks on Fabric

390 To remove crayon marks from clothing or other washable fabrics, first rub the stain well with white vegetable shortening. Then wash the stained area with water and liquid dishwashing detergent.

Felt-Tip-Marker Ink on Skin

391 To remove felt-tip-marker ink from skin, try rubbing with toothpaste and rinsing with water. Repeat the process until the ink disappears.

Ballpoint-Pen Ink on Fabric

392 To get rid of ballpoint-ink stains on fabric, spritz the stain thoroughly with hairspray and rinse it out under warm running water. (Use hairspray in an area away from children.)

More Cleaning Tips

Cleaning Game Cards

393 When game cards get sticky from too much handling, put them into a bag and shake them with talcum powder or baby powder.

Removing Price Stickers

394 Remove stubborn price stickers from plastic or glass containers by rubbing on peanut butter and then washing with water and liquid dishwashing detergent. Repeat until all sticky residue is gone.

Removing Gum From Hair

395 Try using peanut butter or cold cream to remove gum from a child's hair. Then wash the hair as usual to remove the peanut butter or cold cream.

Washing Shower Curtains

396 A plastic shower curtain makes a great floor covering for messy projects. To clean, machine wash the curtain on a gentle cycle, adding ½ cup detergent and ¼ cup bleach. Let the curtain air-dry outside in the sun or indoors on a clothesline.

Display Board Tips

Display Board Substitutes

Plastic-Foam Display Boards

397 Make your own display boards by covering plastic-foam insulation slabs with burlap, felt or large sheets of paper. To make one large display board, place several foam slabs side by side and fasten them together with duct tape. Then attach the covering.

Cardboard Display Board

398 To make a lightweight display board for your room, cover a large piece of corrugated cardboard with a solid color of fabric or wallpaper. Hang the board on a wall. Or use the board as a portable display board.

Impromptu Display Board

399 Cover a chalkboard, a wall or other flat surface with butcher paper, using masking tape as an adhesive. Attach borders, letters and pictures to the butcher paper with removable tape.

Mini-Display Board

400 Use the side of a metal file cabinet as a mini-display board. Encourage your children to attach decorated paper shapes to the metal surface with masking tape. The shapes can be peeled off easily when it's time to put up a new display.

 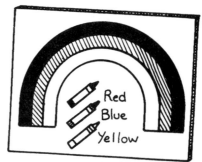

Display Backgrounds

Away With Boring White!

401 Draw more attention to your children's artwork by using brightly colored background paper on your display boards. To cover large areas easily, try colored butcher paper, tablecloths, tissue paper or wrapping paper.

Textured Backgrounds

402 Give your display boards an interesting textured look by using burlap, grass cloth, aluminum foil or nylon net as a background material.

Plastic Tablecloths

403 Cover your large display boards with the thin plastic tablecloths that are sold at party-supply stores. The tablecloths come in a variety of colors and are reusable. After hanging the cloths, you can attach lightweight items with masking tape and print or draw directly on the plastic with permanent felt-tip markers.

Paper Placemats

404 Arrange solid-colored paper placemats on a display board to make an interesting background for your children's artwork. A local restaurant may be willing to donate or sell such placemats to you. Or try purchasing the mats at a restaurant- or party-supply store.

Decorated Paper

405 Let your children decorate butcher paper or plain wrapping paper to make backgrounds for your display boards. Have them try different painting methods such as finger painting, sponge painting, spatter painting or dribble painting.

Hanging Things Up

Tape Tip

406 When hanging up pictures that you do not want marred by thumbtack holes, use removable tape. The tape (available at office-supply stores) can be reused, if desired.

Earring Thumbtacks

407 Start a collection of old or unmatched pierced earrings. They make unique thumbtacks for display boards.

Letters and Borders

Wallpaper Letters

408 Make durable letters for your display boards by cutting them out of wallpaper samples. The letters can be saved and used again to form other words or titles.

Cutting Out Letters

409 Here's a quick trick for cutting the centers out of display board letters such as *O*, *D* or *P*. Instead of piercing the center of a letter and then trying to cut it out, cut right through one side of the letter to cut out the center easily. When the letter is pinned to your display board, the cut will never be noticed.

Letter and Border Match

410 Perk up your display boards by cutting letters and borders out of matching sheets of colorful wrapping paper.

Doily Borders

411 Attach small paper doilies around the edges of a display board to make a lacy border. Decorate the doilies with paper shapes such as hearts in February or colorful flowers in May.

Tube Borders

412 Let your children paint the outsides of cardboard tubes with seasonal colors. When dry, attach the tubes end to end around the edges of a display board for an unusual border.

Handmade Borders

413 Cut strips of construction paper to fit around the edges of a display board. Let your children use rubber stamps, paint, crayons or felt-tip markers to make rows of pumpkins, hearts, bears, numerals, etc., on the paper strips. Then attach the strips to your display board to create a border.

Autumn Leaf Border

414 Gather colorful autumn leaves and crush their stems with the back of a spoon. Place the stems in a mixture of ½ cup water and ⅓ cup glycerin (available at drugstores). Let stand for about one week. Use the beautiful, soft leaves to make an autumn border for a display board.

Adding-Machine Tape Borders

415 Use adding-machine tape (available at office-supply stores) to make display board borders. Let your children make prints on the tape with rubber stamps and commercial ink pads, or cookie cutters dipped in tempera paint.

Preserving Displays

Storing Displays

416 Each time you take down a display board scene, store the pieces in a small plastic trash bag. Group all your small bags together by months or seasons and place them in large plastic trash bags. Clip the large bags to coat hangers with clothespins. Hang the bags on a clothes rod and put dividers between them. When it's time to change a display board, you'll have a whole bagful of scenes to choose from.

See-At-A-Glance Storage

417 Before taking down a display board scene, take a photograph of it. Store the pieces of the display in a large envelope. Glue the photo to the outside of the envelope for easy reference when it's time to put up the display again.

Picture Your Displays

418 Take photographs of your display board scenes before you take them down. Keep the photos in a scrapbook to use as guides for repeating favorite displays.

How Did They Do That?

419 Whenever you visit another school, bring a camera so you can snap photos of special display board scenes. File your snapshots as desired. They'll come in handy when you need new ideas for your own display boards.

Recycling Displays

Reusing Background Paper

420 After taking down the background paper from a display board scene, reuse it. Place the paper on a table, tape the sides down, and let your children freely draw on it with crayons or felt-tip markers.

Reusing Display Board Shapes

421 Remove any staples or pins from your display board shapes. Then use the shapes at your art table for making collages or rubbings.

3-D Display Boards

Move It

422 Use brass paper fasteners to attach arms, legs, tails, etc., to display board figures. You can then change the positions of the movable parts to make the figures appear to be walking, jumping, holding objects, and so forth.

The Real Thing

423 Whenever possible, use real materials in your display board scenes. For instance, attach a real toothbrush for a dental display or empty food boxes for a nutrition display.

Stuff and Puff

424 Cut double shapes of fish, stars or other items from butcher paper. The shapes can be painted, stapled together, and stuffed with crumpled paper or fiberfill to make puffy, three-dimensional display board figures.

Pull It Out

425 Push straight pins in about halfway when hanging a display board scene. Then pull parts of your display out from the board so that they rest against the backs of the pin heads. This will add shadows and depth to your display.

Equipment Tips

Chalkboards

Painted Chalkboards

426 Try making your own chalkboards. Cut pieces of wood or heavy cardboard into shapes such as squares, letters, numerals or animals. Then paint the shapes with chalkboard paint (available at paint stores). Your children can use the chalkboards with chalk for tracing, drawing, writing or learning games.

Plastic-Covered Chalkboards

427 Look in a hardware store for a self-stick plastic covering that has the color and texture of a chalkboard. Create instant chalkboards for your room by attaching the plastic to sturdy cardboard squares, room dividers, cupboard doors or the sides of a bookcase.

Energetic Erasers

428 For chalkboard erasers, provide old large socks that have been washed and dried. Let your children wear the socks like mittens and rub their hands over a chalkboard to erase it.

Dollhouses

Bookshelf Dollhouse

429 An empty shelf in a bookcase can be made into a dollhouse. Just attach wallpaper or self-stick paper to the inside walls and glue on pictures of doors, windows and other decorations. Place a carpet square on the bottom of the shelf, add doll furniture, and you'll be ready for "open house"!

Shoe Box Dollhouse

430 Use shoe boxes with the lids removed to make a dollhouse. Turn the boxes on their sides, stack them as desired, and fasten them together with tape. Decorate the walls of your dollhouse with samples from wallpaper books.

Apartment House

431 Let your children decorate the insides of several shoe boxes to make "apartments." Stack the boxes one on top of the other and secure them with tape to make an apartment building.

Dollhouse Furniture and People

432 Cut small pictures of people and furniture out of old magazines or catalogs. Glue the pictures to the sides of empty thread spools, then stand them inside a dollhouse.

Box Furniture

433 Make dollhouse furniture out of empty boxes. For instance, use a small facial tissue box for a bed or a small cereal box with an opening cut in one side for a television set. Use other kinds of boxes to make tables, chairs and dressers. Attach movable parts, such as controls for a stove, with brass paper fasteners.

Flannelboards

Baby Blanket Flannelboard

434 An old, flannel baby blanket makes a great cover for a flannelboard.

Room Divider Flannelboard

435 A storage container on wheels that serves as a room divider can also be used as a flannelboard. Just attach flannel to the back with a staple gun.

Finger Puppet Flannelboard

436 Find an old fold-up game board (check garage sales or thrift shops). Cover the top surface of the board with flannel and cut a few holes all the way through the board. Then stand the board upright on one side and use it with finger puppets.

School Box Flannelboard

437 Purchase a school box (usually found wherever school supplies are sold). Cover the inside of the hinged lid with blue or green felt. Cut small shapes out of other colors of felt and store them inside the box. Let your children have fun arranging the shapes on the felt-covered box lid.

Flannelboard Substitutes

438 A carpet square or a piece of indoor-outdoor carpeting can be used in place of a flannelboard.

Making Flannelboard Shapes

439 Use felt or flannel to make flannelboard shapes. Or cut shapes out of paper and back them with strips of felt, sandpaper, Velcro or fabric interfacing.

Tippy Flannelboard

440 To keep your flannelboard from tipping over, set it against a painting easel that is not being used. You may even want to make a new flannelboard to specifically fit a particular easel.

Instant Flannelboard

441 Keep a large piece of felt handy. Whenever you are ready to do flannelboard stories or activities, drape the felt over a painting easel.

Storing Flannelboard Pieces

442 Here's an easy way to keep the pieces of each flannelboard activity together. After making the pieces for a song or story, place them in a reclosable plastic bag. Add a card on which you have written the words of the story or song. Then seal the bag and use a permanent felt-tip marker to write the name of the activity on the outside.

Magnet Boards

Magnet Board Fun

443 Use pizza pans or cookie sheets for individual magnet boards.

Cookie Tin Magnet Board

444 Store magnetic shapes or letters inside a large metal cookie tin. Let your children use the lid of the tin as a magnet board.

Decorative Magnets

445 Save magnetic memo holders. The holders can be used with a magnet board for classifying, sorting, counting and matching games.

Making Things Last

Preserving Pictures

446 Preserve pictures and posters that you want to keep from year to year by covering them with clear self-stick paper. The pictures will be easier for your children to handle, and dirt and finger marks can be wiped off easily.

Preserving Learning Games

447 Spray new puzzles and game boards with clear shellac or varnish. They will last much longer. (Work in an area away from children when using shellac or varnish.)

Preserving Game Boxes

448 Game and puzzle boxes often give out before their contents do. To solve this problem, reinforce the boxes with masking tape on the inside corners and transparent tape on the outside corners before letting your children use them.

Perk Up Pencil Erasers

449 You can bring old, hard pencil erasers back to life by rubbing them with sandpaper or an emery board.

No-Rust Wagons

450 To keep wagons that you use outdoors from rusting, drill several small holes in the bottom of each one. When it rains, the water will drain right out.

Room Decorations

Party Plate Decor

451 Brighten your classroom walls by using paper or plastic party plates as teaching aids. For instance, hang three plates in a row with the numeral 3 underneath the row. Or group several plates of the same color together for a color display.

Balloon Decorations

452 Save Mylar gift balloons. Cut an X in the back of each one, then stuff the balloons with tissue paper. After taping the cuts closed, hang the balloons as room decorations for special occasions.

Decorative Doorbell

453 Sew or hot-glue a jingle bell onto a stretchy terry cloth ponytail holder. Slip the holder over your room doorknob. A faint bell sound will alert you whenever the door is opened by a child or a visitor.

Placemat Decor

454 Cloth or plastic placemats with pictures on them make nice classroom decorations for walls or bulletin boards. Some placemats are printed with alphabet letters or maps, making them fun learning aids.

Wall Calendar Numerals

455 If your room calendar hangs on a wall and you can't attach dates with pins or thumbtacks, use little squares pulled from self-stick note pads. Just write numerals on the squares as needed and stick them in the appropriate spaces on your calendar.

Pop Bottle Vase

456 Use a large, plastic soft-drink bottle as a vase. Just rinse out the bottle, discard the cap, and remove the label. If desired, decorate the bottle with permanent felt-tip marker designs, shiny stickers or glued-on pieces of colored tissue paper.

Sand Table Tips

Sand Play

457 To add interest to your sand area, include wet sand as well as dry sand. Let your children explore and experiment with the similarities and differences.

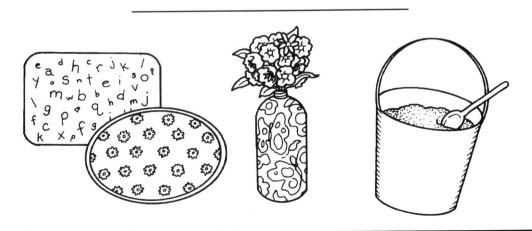

Sand Comb

458 For a fun sand toy, let your children use a large, plastic hair lifter (available at drugstores). Encourage them to use the lifter to "comb" designs in the sand.

Sand Scoops

459 The plastic measuring scoops that come in boxes of powdered laundry detergent make perfect sand toys for little hands.

Sand Area Cleanup

460 Place a small broom and dustpan next to the sand table for your children to use. This will encourage them to help clean up after sand area activities.

Tents

Homemade Tents

461 Old bedspreads are perfect for making tents. Drape one over a table inside your room or over a clothes-line outdoors.

No-Slip Tents

462 When draping a sheet or blanket over a piece of furniture to make a tent, keep it from slipping off by securing it with A-clamps (available at hardware stores). The clamps are much safer to use than books or other heavy objects.

Toys

Simple Pull Toy

463 Punch a hole close to an edge of a paper plate and tie on a piece of string or yarn. Let a child pull the plate across the floor as a pull toy. Small objects can be placed on the plate, if desired.

Homemade Dolls

464 Save different sizes of liquid dishwashing detergent bottles. Turn the bottles into dolls by adding faces, clothing, hair, etc., with felt-tip markers.

Toy Parking Garage

465 Use a cardboard box that is divided into compartments to make a parking garage for toy cars.

Bread Box Garages

466 Check thrift shops or garage sales for old bread boxes. They make great garages for toy cars and trucks.

Tiny Toy Tip

467 Tiny toys will always be easy to locate if you keep them stored in the pockets of clear-plastic shoe bags.

Storing Outdoor Toys

468 Want to keep your outdoor toys in an accessible place yet out of sight? Try storing pieces of smaller equipment, such as plastic balls, bats, ring-toss game pieces and scooter boards, in a laundry hamper with a lid.

Something New

469 To stimulate learning, always keep some toys in storage so you can occasionally add something new to your room.

Toy Rotation

470 Keep your children's interest alive by rotating toys and games among the rooms of your teaching center.

Toy Party

471 Encourage recycling by holding a toy party. Ask your children to select old, usable toys at home that they no longer want. Have them wrap their toys in newspaper before bringing them in. Ask parents to write their children's names on the packages and to indicate whether a toy is appropriate for a boy or a girl. Distribute the wrapped gifts at your party. Each child will be happy to go home with a "new" toy. (Have a few extra wrapped toys on hand in case they are needed.)

Water Table Tips

Colored Water

472 Use this idea to make water play more fun. Fill a plastic dishpan halfway with warm water. Then add drops of food coloring and a small squirt of liquid dishwashing detergent.

Scented Water

473 For a different kind of experience, add a small amount of scented shampoo to your water table. Your children will find this especially relaxing if you use warm water instead of cold water.

Under the Sea

474 Add interest to your water table by lining the bottom with a waterproof, plastic aquarium background that has pictures of undersea plant life. Add some real shells, if desired.

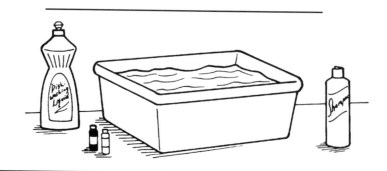

Squirt Toy

475 Purchase a nasal aspirator (available at drugstores). Let your children use the aspirator as a squirt toy at your water table.

Sprinklers

476 Let your children use small cookie-sprinkle containers with perforated lids as water toys. Encourage them to fill the containers with water and then turn them upside down to create "showers."

Storing Water Toys

477 Keep a mesh bag handy for storing water toys. The bag allows toys to drain and dry quickly when water play is finished.

Tactile Learning Fun

478 Place two tubs inside your empty water table. Put different materials into each tub, such as sand and rice, or water and wood chips. This will provide your children with two tactile learning experiences at the same time.

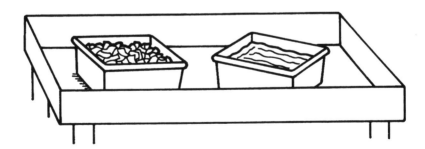

Shower Curtain Floor Covering

479 Place a plastic shower curtain under your water table to catch spills.

Carpeting Trick

480 A piece of inexpensive indoor-outdoor carpeting under your water table will take care of spills and slips. The carpeting dries quickly and is easy to clean.

Bring Out the Bath Mats

481 Place rubber bath mats (the kind with suction cups) on the floor where your children stand when they do water play. This will give their feet traction and help prevent slips.

Good Earth Tips

Fast-Food Recyclables

French Fry Holders

482 Save French fry holders and attach them to a bulletin board for pockets.

Beverage Trays

483 Cardboard beverage trays are great to use for carrying paints or other supplies to and from a work area.

Stirring Sticks

484 Collect colored plastic stirring sticks to use as counters for math games.

Cream Cups

485 Small cream cups can be used as individual holders for glue or glitter.

Paper Bags

486 Save colorful paper bags from fast-food restaurant meals. Use them again when it's time to pack lunches for a picnic.

Hamburger Containers

487 Empty hamburger containers make perfect holders for bird nests and other fragile objects. Or use them as boxes when wrapping small gifts and surprises.

Salad Containers

488 Clear-plastic salad containers can be used as mini-greenhouses for sprouting seeds. Or turn the containers into small terrariums.

Room Tips

Multipurpose Recyclables

Gallon Milk Jugs

489 Cut plastic gallon milk jugs in half. Use the bottoms as planters, snack bowls, crayon holders or molds for plaster-of-Paris art. Use the tops for sand or water funnels, megaphones, plastic-foam ball scoops or yarn holders.

Panty Hose

490 Old, clean panty hose can be used for different purposes: the elastic tops make extra-large rubber bands; three cut-off legs are great for braiding; one cut-off leg can hold small water toys; squares of the nylon fabric make perfect covers for insect jars or jars used for growing alfalfa sprouts.

Mouthwash Bottle Caps

491 Save the tall, white caps from large bottles of mouthwash. Use them as juice cups, seed planters, water toys, sand toys or doll dishes.

Fabric Softener Sheets

492 When you take fabric softener sheets out of a dryer, iron them flat. Use them in place of interfacing for small craft projects. Or tie herbs inside the sheets to make scented bath bags for gifts.

Plastic Bags

493 Save plastic grocery bags and other plastic sacks from stores. Use them for distributing take-home materials or enclosing not-quite-dry artwork at dismissal time. The bags are also handy for holding soiled or damp clothing.

Paper Towel Tips

Paper Towel Alternative

494 Whenever possible, use cloth towels instead of paper towels for cleaning up spills. You'll help save trees and cut down on trash at the same time.

A Better Paper Towel

495 For times when you feel paper towels are necessary, consider using the blue automotive-care towels that are found at gas stations. They are very strong and absorbent, so you'll end up using fewer of them. Check at a local gas station to find out where to purchase the towels.

Recycling

Recycled Paper

496 Keep a box in your room where the children can throw away papers that have one clean side. Stack, cut and staple the papers to make small notepads for your group.

Which Is Which?

497 To help your children remember which kinds of paper can be recycled and which cannot, tape examples of recyclable paper (construction paper, typing paper, etc.) to one wastebasket and examples of non-recyclable paper (facial tissues, paper napkins, etc.) to another.

Save a Tree

498 Use this concrete example to help your children understand why recycling is important. Together, measure a 3-foot stack of old newspapers. Explain that by recycling the stack, you will help save one tree from being cut down and turned into paper.

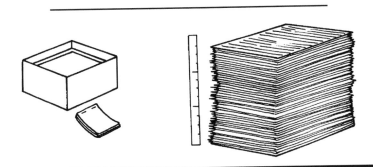

Recycling a Bottle Cap

499 Try using an old pop bottle cap to fix a chair that is tippy because it is missing the little setting at the bottom of a leg. Use a hot glue gun to attach the bottle cap to the chair leg. Wait 30 seconds and turn the chair upright. Test the chair to see if it is stable. If it is not, pull the bottle cap off before the glue has fully hardened. Then add more glue or put a small piece of cardboard inside the cap and try again.

Paper Bag Drawing Pads

500 Here's one way to recycle brown paper grocery bags. Cut them into squares of equal size. Then make drawing pads for your children by stacking the squares, printed sides down, and stapling them together along one side.

Recycling Station

501 Set out painted boxes, clearly labeled, to collect recyclable items such as glass, cans and paper. Encourage your children to bring these items from home and place them in the appropriate boxes. Take the filled boxes to a recycling center and use the money you receive to purchase materials for your program.

Book Swap

502 Encourage your children to reuse books by having a book-swap day. Have them bring in books that they no longer want. Give them one chip for each book they bring. Arrange all the books on shelves and tables. Let the children look through the books and use their chips to buy the ones they want—one chip per book.

Goodwill Day

503 Have your children bring in toys they no longer want but are still in good working order to give to needy children in your area. If possible, let your children help take the toys to the place where they will be distributed.

More Good Earth Tips

Self-Stick Note Savers

504 Try cutting whole self-stick note papers in half so that each piece has a sticky end. By using these narrower notes, you'll save money as well as paper.

Show As Well As Tell

505 Demonstrate to your children how you use resources wisely (turn off lights when you leave a room, do not let water run while you wash dishes, don't ride when you can walk, etc.). Then explain what you are doing and why. Showing as well as telling will make a stronger impression on your children.

Guidance Tips

Awards

Game Prizes

506 Simple items make great prizes for games. Try using stickers, small boxes of raisins, balloons, crayons, sugarless gum or small packages of nuts.

Freebies

507 Many free items are available that can be used for awards. Examples include prizes from cereal boxes, stamplike stickers from junk mail, and baseball or animal cards that come with food products.

Homemade Awards

508 Try making items to use for special awards or prizes. Your children will love receiving treats such as seasonal shape cutouts, simple finger puppets, stick puppets, jingle-bell bracelets or decorated paper crowns.

Seasonal Napkins

509 Look for seasonal paper napkins in supermarkets or party-supply stores. Keep the colorful napkins handy to use for awards at special times.

Behavior Tips

Punching Out Stress

510 Help your children release feelings of stress or anger by providing them with a special pillow to use as a punching bag.

Tearing Newspaper

511 For young children, tearing newspaper is an excellent way to release the tense energy build-up that often accompanies anger. Afterward, the children can help with the newspaper cleanup.

Playing Out Stress

512 When your children become stressed or angry, provide them with dolls or other toys. Encourage them to use the toys like puppets to act out their feelings.

Shaving Cream Soother

513 In times of stress, playing with shaving cream can have a calming effect on young children. A little water is all it takes for easy cleanup.

Running Off Energy

514 Outdoor treasure hunts provide a good way to help young children run off excess energy. Try hiding small prizes or seasonal treats in a yard or a play area. Make sure each child finds a treasure.

Stuffed Animal Listeners

515 Seat one or two stuffed animals in a corner to be special "listeners." When your children are arguing or fighting, try redirecting their energy by having them talk to the stuffed animals about their feelings.

Determining Fair Turns

516 To determine how long "fair turns" should last, use an hourglass egg timer. When your children learn how to use the timer themselves, you won't be called upon constantly to say when a turn is over.

Riding Toy Turns

517 To reduce arguments about taking turns on riding toys, play music while your children are using them. Make a rule that whenever a song ends, a child on a riding toy must give another child a turn.

Keeping Things Equal

518 If two children are fighting over something that can be divided, try this. Let one child divide the item or items in half. Then let the other child be first to choose the half that he or she wants.

Slowing Down the Action

519 When playing active games indoors, young children often become excited and bump into one another. To slow down the action, have them drop down on their hands and knees and crawl. Or have them sit and scoot around the floor on their bottoms.

Flying Toy Times

520 When young children play with airplanes or other flying toys, they can get carried away and start running around the room. To prevent this, make a rule that the children must either be seated or kneeling when playing with flying toys.

Developing Self-Esteem

Puppet Talk

521 Shy children may find it easier to express themselves through a puppet when they speak. Make a hand puppet out of an old sock or a paper bag and give it to a child. Then ask the child questions for the "puppet" to answer.

Say Something Positive

522 You can help develop your children's self-esteem by saying positive things about them. To make sure that you don't forget anyone, try this. Make a list of your children's names and slide it into a magnetic photo page. Tape the page closed. Then use a washable felt-tip marker to keep a daily record of positive statements you make. At the end of each day, just wipe the photo page clean.

Feelings Chart

523 On a large posterboard square, glue pictures of people expressing different emotions such as happiness, sadness and anger. Cover the square with clear self-stick paper. Each day have your children circle faces on the chart with washable felt-tip markers to indicate how they are feeling.

Feel-Good Badges

524 Cut seasonal shapes from stiff paper and label them with positive statements such as "I share with others" or "I put away my toys." Tape safety pins to the backs of the shapes. Whenever a child does something positive, acknowledge it by letting the child wear the appropriate badge.

See What I Can Do!

525 If you have access to a copy machine, let your children experience the thrill of making copies of their work. Being able to share their pictures and beginning writing attempts with family members and friends will make them feel very special.

Praise Works Best

526 Instead of always correcting rule breakers, keep an eye out for children who are doing what has been asked of them. Heap on the praise with comments such as "Andrew is doing such a good job putting away the toys." Then watch your children's pride blossom.

Sharing Nice Thoughts

527 At week's end, give each child a chance to say something nice to or about another group member; for example, "Thank you, Ashley, for sharing your crayons with me," or "Cody helped me put the blocks away." Hearing positive comments like these will help your children feel good about themselves as they leave for the weekend. Be sure to add comments, if necessary, so that everyone gets mentioned.

Get-Well Card

528 Whenever one of your children is absent because of illness, let the other children make a group get-well card to mail or deliver by hand. Knowing that others care will help the child at home feel special.

Getting Acquainted

Group Photo Display

529 Help everyone get acquainted at the beginning of the year by putting up a bulletin board display that includes your children's photographs and their names.

Self-Portraits

530 At the beginning of the year, let your children decorate paper plates with collage materials to create self-portraits. Attach name tags and display the plates on a wall. Use the self-portraits to start a discussion about new names and faces.

I Know You!

531 Here's a fun way to help your children learn to recognize one another. Place a photograph of each child in a hat. Then let the children take turns drawing a photo from the hat, finding the child pictured in the photo, and giving the photo to that child.

Shine Like a Star

532 To help your children become better acquainted, substitute their names when you sing familiar songs. *The Muffin Man* of *Drury Lane* could become *Melissa Jones* of *White Oak Street*, or *Yankee Doodle* could become *Michael Fisher*. Using this technique gives every child a chance to be a star and shine.

Name Recognition

533 To help your children with name recognition, sit in a circle and place a small blanket loosely over a child's head. Then sing the song below and let the other children fill in the blank. Repeat for each child.

Sung to: "Ten Little Indians"

Who, oh, who is under the blanket?
Who, oh, who is under the blanket?
Who, oh, who is under the blanket?
I know who! It's _____.

Nancy Hartman

Puzzle Pals

534 For this get-acquainted game, start with one posterboard square for every two children. Cut the squares in half in different ways, mix up the pieces, and hand them out. Let the children match up their puzzle pieces with one another to find their "puzzle pals."

Choosing Partners

535 To help ensure that your children rotate partners for games and other activities, try this. Put photographs of half your group into a hat and let the other half draw photos when choosing partners. Alternate the procedure each time partners are chosen.

Let Me Introduce Myself

536 Whenever a new child joins your group, ask everyone in turn to stand and introduce him or herself. This way, the new child won't feel that he or she is being singled out.

Setting Routines

Starting the Day

537 At the beginning of the school day, greet each child at the door, if possible. This will help the children feel welcome and eager to learn.

Picture Chart

538 Young children need to know that their day will be predictable. Post a picture chart illustrating the day's activities in sequence. Go over the chart with your group.

Activity Clothesline

539 Hang pictures of the day's activities in sequence on a clothesline at the children's eye level. As your children complete the activities, they can take the pictures off the line.

Bridging the Gap

540 Help your children feel secure about starting new tasks. As you end each activity, explain to them what the group will be doing next.

See You Tomorrow

541 As your children prepare to go home, take time to discuss the day's activities and talk about what will happen on the following day. This will help the children begin to understand the school-day routine and make them look forward to coming back.

More Guidance Tips

Getting Attention

542 Try whispering instead of speaking in a loud voice when you want to get your children's attention. They'll usually quiet down fast in case they might be missing something!

Offer Specific Choices

543 Making choices can sometimes be difficult for young children. Instead of asking a general question (such as "What toy do you want to play with?"), try offering just two choices (such as "Do you want to play with the wagon or the truck?").

Changing the Environment

544 If your children consistently display unwanted behavior, check to see if changing your room environment will help. For instance, try relocating your block area if the children frequently knock over block structures.

How Am I Doing?

545 Let your children play-act being the teacher once in awhile. Listen to what they say and how they say it to get an idea of how they perceive you. Check to see if they are learning what you think you have been teaching. You may be surprised!

Health and Safety Tips

First Aid

Sponge Cold Pack

546 Store a wet sponge in a freezer to use as a cold pack. It's easier for little hands to hold than an ice cube.

Dripless Cold Pack

547 Make an easy-to-hold, dripless cold pack for bumped foreheads and cut lips by filling a plastic pill bottle almost to the top with water and placing it in a freezer.

Washcloth Cold Pack

548 A damp washcloth kept in a freezer makes a good cold pack for swellings and bruises.

Ice Substitute Cold Pack

549 Store a small package of ice substitute in a freezer for using on bumps and bruises. It's less messy and easier to hold than ice. If desired, make a pocket for the ice substitute out of colorful washcloths.

Frozen Treat First Aid

550 For reducing the swelling of a bruised lip, try giving a child a frozen fruit treat to eat. This can be more appealing than using a cold pack.

Removing Splinters

551 Removing a hard-to-see splinter will be easier if you darken it first by applying a little iodine to the area.

Red Washcloth Hint

552 Keep a red or maroon washcloth on hand to use for washing cuts and scrapes. The color of the cloth acts as camouflage, preventing children from becoming panicked by the sight of their own blood.

Small First-Aid Kit

553 Use an empty disposable-wipe container with a lid to make a small first-aid kit.

Complete First-Aid Kit

554 Make a first-aid kit for your room that includes the following items: adhesive tape, sterile pads, small bandages, an elastic bandage, soap, antiseptic cream, thermometer, scissors, tweezers, safety pins, chemical ice pack, syrup of ipecac, painkillers (liquid acetaminophen for infants and young children; chewable acetaminophen tablets for older children). Place the items and emergency telephone numbers (doctors, hospital, poison control center, etc.) in a secure box with a childproof lock.

Backpack First-Aid Kit

555 Make a first-aid kit out of a backpack. Hang the kit on a hook in a visible spot in your room, out of the children's reach. The backpack is especially convenient for taking along on field trips.

Health and Hygiene

Toothbrushes

556 To help your children locate their own toothbrushes, put masking tape on the backs of plastic holders and write the children's names on the tape. Have the children dry off their toothbrushes after brushing and replace them in their holders. Check at the end of each week to see if the holders need cleaning.

Soap Tip

557 If the bar of soap in your room is old and covered with dark cracks, toss it out. Chances are it's harboring and spreading germs rather than preventing them. Replace the soap with a fresh bar or a pump-type liquid soap dispenser.

Toothbrush Holder

558 For a handy toothbrush holder, invert a green plastic berry basket. The handles of your children's toothbrushes will fit nicely through the spaces in the bottom of the basket.

Soap-In-A-Sock

559 Your children will always have soap available for washing hands if you place the bar in an old knee-high nylon and tie the stocking to your sink faucet. This will also help prevent mess.

Child-Proof Towel

560 Here's a way to keep your children's hand towel from falling on the floor after use. Hang the towel over a rod, then fasten the ends of the towel together with safety pins.

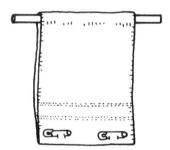

Soothing Hand Lotion

561 To sooth your children's hands after repetitive washings, purchase a bottle of Corn Husker's Lotion (available in large drugstores). The lotion is non-greasy, absorbs quickly, and doesn't sting when applied to chapped hands.

Safety

No-Choke Testing Tube

562 Use a hot glue gun to affix a No-Choke Testing Tube to the inside of a handy cabinet door. Whenever you notice a suspiciously small toy or other object in your room, you can test it in the tube immediately to see if it presents a choking hazard. No-Choke Testing Tubes are available through Toys to Grow On, P.O. Box 17, Long Beach, CA 90801; 1-800-542-8338.

Clothespin Clips

563 Clip together story patterns, bulletin board pieces, etc., with colorful plastic clothespins rather than small, easy-to-swallow paper clips.

Safety Cord Cover

564 Use a paper-towel tube to make a safety cover for an electrical cord that's too long. First, wind up the slack in the cord and secure it with a twist tie. Then cover it with the cardboard tube to keep little hands away from danger.

Sliding Glass Doors

565 Do you have sliding glass doors in your teaching area? If so, attach colorful decals to prevent your children from accidentally walking into the glass.

Red Means Hot

566 Use nail polish to paint a red dot on the hot water faucet of your room sink. Your children will be less likely to turn on the hot water by mistake.

Mr. Yuk Stickers

567 Call your local poison control center to find out where you can get Mr. Yuk stickers. Use the stickers to teach your children that they should never taste, eat or touch anything that has Mr. Yuk's face on it.

Fire Safety

568 Choose two different routes for getting out of your room or building in case of fire. Hold fire drills periodically so your children learn the two ways to exit.

Food Jar Safety

569 When opening a jar of food that has a safety pop-top, listen for the popping sound. If the lid doesn't pop, throw out the food—the jar may have been previously opened.

Play Area Safety

570 Remember to re-childproof the areas your toddlers play in as their skills and interests change.

Management Tips

Helpers

Helper Cards

571 Organize your helper list by writing the name of each child on a small index card. Put the cards on a ring and flip them over one at a time when choosing classroom helpers. This way the shy child will not be left out, and your children will learn to recognize one another's names as you read them off the cards.

Helper Necklaces

572 Classroom helpers are sure to remember their tasks if you string cleanup cards on loops of yarn for them to wear as necklaces. Put the necklaces in a basket each morning and let your children choose the ones they want to wear that day.

Helper Game

573 When choosing a helper, play a game of Detective. First, run your finger up and down a list of your children's names and stop beside one of them. Then have the children try guessing the name as you give clues such as these: "My helper is a boy. He has black hair. He is wearing brown pants and a green shirt. His name begins with the letter *D*." Your children will love this game and won't realize how much they are learning while playing it.

Helper Sticks

574 To avoid always choosing the same children as helpers, try this. Print each child's name on a separate craft stick and place the sticks in a can or a jar. Whenever you need a special helper, randomly select a stick from the can.

Door Helper

575 To prevent a mass flow to and from your room, appoint a child to act as door helper. The helper can assist in lining up the other children, counting noses, and holding the door open.

Important Helpers

576 Choose daily helpers to water the plants and feed the fish or other animals. Stress the importance of these jobs and use them to help your children develop a sense of responsibility.

Helper of the Day

577 Take an instant photograph of each child and place it in a basket. Each morning, choose one of the photos and post it on a wall to indicate the helper of the day. Keep chosen photos in a special pile until all of the children have had a chance to be the helper of the day. Then mix them all up and start again.

Helper Poster

578 Choose a name for your group, such as Huggy Bears. For each child, cut a bear shape out of colorful paper and print the child's name on it. Attach all the bear shapes to a large piece of construction paper and hang it on a bulletin board. When it's time to choose the helper of the day, pin a star on one of the bear shapes.

3-D Helper Chart

579 To assign helpers for passing out different items, make this easy-to-read chart. Across the top of a piece of posterboard, attach an example of each item to be passed out (a paper cup, a plastic spoon, a small pair of scissors, a piece of art paper, etc.). Under each item, glue a spring-type clothespin. Print each helper's name on a card and clip it under an item on the chart.

Helper Picture Chart

580 Make a chart that includes pictures of tasks that your helpers do each day. Print each child's name on a separate spring-type clothespin. Every morning, clip the clothespins to the pictures and have the children look for their names to discover how they will be helping that day.

Shoe-Bag Helper Chart

581 Use a hanging shoe bag with pockets to make a helper chart. Label the pockets with the names of tasks and insert cards with your children's names on them in the pockets.

Lost and Found

Flagging Pencils

582 To help your children keep track of their pencils, try this. Print each child's name on a piece of masking tape and attach it to the child's pencil in the shape of a flag.

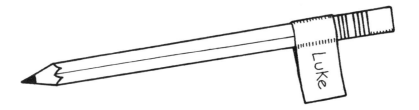

Toy and Game Parts Box

583 Throughout the day, it's inevitable that odd parts of toys and games will turn up around the room. Instead of returning them to their proper places each time, make a special container just for toy and game parts. Not only will this save time, you'll always know where to look if a part is missing.

Name Tags

Wallpaper Name Tags

584 To make colorful name tags, cut shapes out of wallpaper samples. Use a permanent felt-tip marker to print your children's names on the tags.

Fabric Name Tags

585 Laminate a piece of fabric that contains a pattern of animals, toys, etc. Cut the fabric into name-tag-size squares, each containing a pattern picture. Use a permanent felt-tip marker to print each child's name on a tag and cut small holes in the tops for inserting safety pins.

Alphabet Noodle Name Tags

586 Print each child's name in upper-case letters on a separate self-stick name tag. Set out uncooked alphabet noodles. Let your children sort through the noodles to find the letters that make up their names. Then have them glue the noodles on top of the matching letters on their name tags. When the glue is dry, let your children peel the backs off the self-stick tags and wear them.

Note Pad Name Tags

587 Find a small note pad that is cut into an animal shape (or any appropriate shape). Make name tags by gluing pages from the note pad onto squares or circles cut from posterboard. Print your children's names on the tags. Laminate the tags, if desired, then punch a hole in the top of each one. Lace yarn through the holes for tying into necklaces.

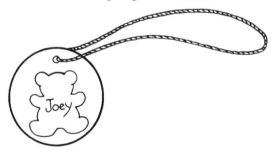

Self-Stick-Paper Name Tags

588 Cut seasonal shapes out of colored or patterned self-stick paper. Print your children's names on the shapes with a permanent felt-tip marker. When it's time to use the name tags, peel off the backing and stick the tags on your children's shirts or jackets.

Greeting Card Name Tags

589 Cut basic shapes, such as rectangles, circles or stars, out of the fronts of old greeting cards. Use a permanent felt-tip marker to print a child's name on each shape. Punch a hole in the top of each shape for inserting a safety pin.

Reusable Name Tags

590 Make name tags that can be used year after year by cutting out posterboard shapes, covering them with clear self-stick paper, and punching holes in the tops for inserting safety pins. To label the tags, attach strips of masking tape with the children's names printed on them. At the end of the school year, peel off the tape strips and attach new ones.

Picture Postcard Name Tags

591 Use old picture postcards as name tags when you go on a field trip to the post office. Attach strips of masking tape or white artist's tape to the picture sides of the cards and print your center's name on the tape with a permanent felt-tip marker. Then attach safety pins to the backs of the postcards.

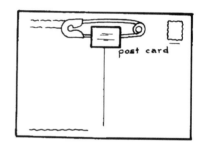

Springtime Name Tags

592 Ask parents to save empty seed packages for you. Use the packages to make name tags when your children are learning about growing flowers and vegetables.

Color Name Tags

593 When your children are learning about colors, make name tags out of Formica samples or paint strips (both available at hardware stores).

Brown Paper Name Tags

594 When you take your children on a field trip to a supermarket, make name tags for them to wear by cutting shapes out of brown paper grocery bags.

Personal Tips

Personal Belongings

595 It's inevitable that you will have some items in your room that you don't want your children to handle. As a precautionary measure, always have at least one drawer with a childproof latch or lock.

Personal Books

596 Stamp your own name or the name of your teaching center in personal books. This will keep them from getting mixed up with library books.

Teacher Attire

597 Try wearing colorful prints to work whenever possible. They are eye-catching and interesting to look at, thus perfect for attracting children's attention. Prints also are great for hiding spots and stains.

Substitute Teacher Tips

Sing-Along Help

598 Tape-record the songs you sing at circle time and at dismissal. A substitute teacher can then play the tape, sing along, and feel confident that he or she has the correct words and tunes.

Sticker Motivators

599 Keep a sticker collection in your substitute-teacher file to be used as motivators, if needed. Be sure to check and replenish the collection after each use.

Photo Name Tags

600 Glue a photo of each child's face on a name-tag shape cut from posterboard. Print each child's name under his or her picture and tie on loops of yarn for hangers. The photo name tags can help a substitute teacher quickly match the children's names with their faces.

Time Savers

Paper Shapes in a Jiffy

601 Make paper shapes for your group in a jiffy by always cutting out four, six or eight at a time.

Duplicating Patterns

602 When duplicating a pattern on a copy machine, use colored paper instead of white to avoid having to color the copies by hand later. For instance, use brown paper for a bear pattern or red paper for an apple pattern.

Copying Photos

603 Avoid having to stop and take your children's photos every time you need them for name tags, helper charts, gifts, etc. At the beginning of the school year, take a close-up photo of each of the children. Then use a copy machine to make duplicates of the photos. Keep these photo copies handy to use as needed.

Easy Transfers

604 Use black-and-white pictures from coloring books to make your own transfers. Just duplicate a picture on a copy machine, place the copy face down on paper or fabric, and press with a warm iron. With some machines, you can even enlarge the picture to any size you want before transferring it to a song chart or a homemade poster. Use felt-tip markers or paint to color the transferred picture.

White Pencil Trick

605 When tracing around shapes or printing words on colored construction paper, use a white pencil to do the job.

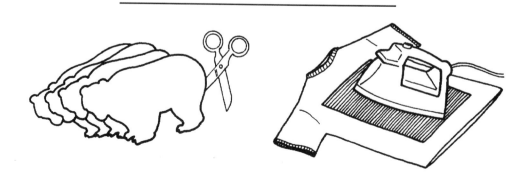

Quick-Dry Trick

606 Keep a hair dryer handy in your desk drawer. Use it for drying clean, damp spots on fabric and paintings that are almost dry (not wet) and ready to be taken home.

See-At-A-Glance Class List

607 Make a see-at-a-glance class list to use for keeping track of your children on the playground or a field trip. Trace the outline of a large key-ring decoration on an index card. Cut out the shape and print your class list in small letters on the card. Glue the card to the decoration and cover both the card and decoration with self-stick paper before attaching to your key ring.

Visitors

Thank-You Booklet

608 When you invite a community helper or other guest to visit your room, take photographs of the person doing activities with your children. For a special thank you, make copies of the photos and send them to your guest in a decorated booklet.

Organization Tips

Desk-Top Organization

Colorful File Box

609 Use a large, narrow detergent box to make a file box for holding professional magazines or papers. Cut off the top part of the box diagonally and discard it. Then cover the bottom part of the box with colorful self-stick paper.

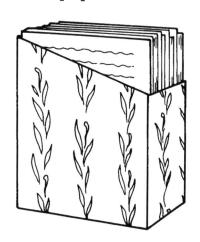

Recipes for Learning

610 Keep a recipe file box on your desk. Each time you find a recipe for learning materials, such as clay, sand mixes or playdough, copy it on an index card and file it in your recipe box. You'll always have the information at your fingertips.

Organizing and Storing Materials

Construction Paper Storage

611 To keep construction paper sorted by colors and easily accessible, store it in stacked in–out baskets (the kind used on desk tops and available at office-supply stores).

Homemade Storage Boxes

612 Cut one end off of each of several boxes that are the same size. Stack the boxes one on top of the other to make holders for different colors of construction paper.

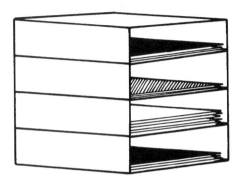

Yarn Storage Boxes

613 Store different colors of yarn in cardboard boxes that are divided into compartments. These kinds of boxes are often given away at places that sell bottled goods.

Net Yarn Bag

614 Place balls of yarn in a net onion bag and pull the ends out through the holes as needed.

No More Yarn Tangles

615 Here's an easy way to store yarn so that it remains tangle-free while you are using it. Place the skein in a clear plastic bag, punch a hole in a bottom corner, and pull out the yarn end. Close the top of the bag with a twist tie.

Storing Rickrack

616 Organize and store rickrack, elastic and ribbon pieces by wrapping them around empty thread spools.

String Holder

617 Use an old kitchen funnel to hold a ball of string. Just place the ball inside the funnel and pull the string end out of the spout.

Storing Rolls of Paper

618 For organizing and storing rolls of giftwrap, foil, waxed paper, etc., use extra-large soft-drink cartons.

Crepe Paper Holder

619 Mount a round curtain rod on a wall or under a counter top. Use the rod for organizing and hanging rolls of colored crepe-paper streamers. Just run the rod through the centers of the rolls and secure it in place. Then pull down and cut off streamers as needed.

Rubber Band Holders

620 Paint toilet-tissue tubes the same colors as the rubber bands you use. Your children can help store the bands by wrapping them around the matching-colored tubes.

Card Game Containers

621 Store the cards for different games in plastic or metal bandage boxes. For easy identification, glue picture labels on the fronts of the boxes.

Plastic Lid Storage

622 Place an old dish drainer inside a cupboard for organizing and storing different sizes of plastic lids.

Organizing Nuts and Bolts

623 Organize and store different sizes of nuts, bolts, screws, etc., in tuna fish cans. Smooth rough edges on the cans before use.

Storage Containers

Old Envelopes

624 Use old envelopes for storing flat items such as flannel-board cutouts, display board letters or colored paper scraps. Just cross out any writing on the envelopes and add new labels.

Shoe Bag Storage

625 Hang a shoe bag with pockets in your room for storing small materials such as crayons, scissors, clothespins and craft sticks.

Coffee Can Cubbies

626 Spray-paint coffee cans in an area away from the children. When dry, glue the cans together side by side or in pyramid shapes. Place the cans on a shelf, with the open ends facing out, to use for storage.

Disposable-Wipe Containers

627 Ask parents who have infants to save empty disposable-wipe containers for you. The plastic boxes come with hinged lids and are great for storing small things such as felt-tip markers or game pieces.

Travel Soap Box

628 Look in a drugstore for a travel soap-bar case with a lid. The plastic box can be used to store small items such as stickers, paper clips or crayons.

Art Portfolio

629 Use a cardboard art portfolio to store and transport large items such as posters, bulletin board pieces or Big Books. The cardboard portfolios are available at art and stationery stores.

Ice-Cream Tubs

630 One-gallon, plastic ice-cream tubs with lids make great storage containers for odds and ends. Label the containers clearly and stack them on shelves for easy access.

Video Cassette Boxes

631 Use empty video cassette boxes to store easy-to-lose items such as math counters or small manipulatives.

Cardboard Pet Carriers

632 Cardboard pet carriers (available at pet stores and veterinary clinics) are handy for storing and toting games, toys and other materials. The carriers are relatively inexpensive and will last a long time.

Hardware Storage Box

633 Use a hardware storage box with small drawers for holding small items such as paper clips, reinforcement circles and erasers.

Tackle Box

634 A plastic tackle box makes a great container for a child to store personal items such as crayons, glue and scissors. If desired, help the child to personalize the box by decorating the outside.

Parent Communication Tips

Parent and Student Folders

Parent Folders

635 At the beginning of the year, distribute your informational handouts to each parent in a brightly colored folder or binder. As the year progresses, parents can insert additional handouts into the folders or binders, thus keeping all pertinent information together.

Student Folders

636 When school begins, start a folder for each of your children. Over time, add the children's self-portraits, their heights and weights, their favorite paintings, their beginning handwriting samples, etc. You'll find that the folders are perfect to use as progress charts at parent conference time.

New-Student File

637 Always make a few extra copies of commonly used paperwork such as newsletters, name-tag blanks, school supplies lists and letters to parents. Put these copies in a new-student file. When a new child joins your group, it will be easy to compile the information and promptly send it home.

Parent Memos

Parent Bulletin Board

638 Place your parent bulletin board by the entrance of your room to ensure greater visibility.

Frame It

639 Whenever you have a special memo you want parents to notice, frame it in a cardboard portrait mat or slip it into a picture frame before posting it in your room.

Shoe-Bag Mailbox

640 Important notices and letters for parents often fall off cubby shelves and are lost. To solve this problem, use a shoe bag with pockets to make a parent "mailbox." Label each pocket with a parent's name and have mothers or fathers check daily for their "mail."

Necklace Messages

641 Use a felt-tip marker to write important messages to parents on cut-out paper shapes. Punch holes in the shapes and string them on loops of yarn for the children to wear as necklaces when they go home.

Parent Newsletters

Friday Letter

642 Communicate with parents each week by sending home a "Friday Letter." Include information about the week's happenings such as topics studied, field trips and appropriate quotes from the children. On the last Friday of each month, attach a calendar of events for the next month. Parents will look forward to receiving their newsletter each Friday.

Newsletter Illustrations

643 Ask local newspapers to donate old clip-art books. Cut seasonal pictures, designs and borders from the books to use for decorating the pages of your parent newsletters.

More Parent Communication Tips

Wish List

644 Send home a list of items you need for your room and ask parents to donate them throughout the year. Your requests might range from simple throw-aways (such as egg cartons, yogurt containers or plastic lids) to large items (such as a toaster oven or an electric frying pan for cooking activities).

Notes From Parents

645 When parents send notes asking that their children not play outdoors or explaining new arrangements for after-school pickups, post the notes on a memo board by your door. The notes will serve as reminders whenever you have your children prepare to leave the room.

Advertising Brochures

646 Most hospitals put together a "new family" packet for local distribution. Ask to have your teaching center brochure included. Also ask to leave copies of your brochure in pediatricians' offices.

Tiny Tot Tips

Diapering and Dressing

Changing Mats

647 Cut plastic curtains into squares and use them for diaper-changing mats.

Hand Puppet Fun

648 When changing a baby's diaper, wear a sock puppet on one hand. The child will tend to lie still when his or her attention is focused on the puppet.

Easy Dressing

649 When toddlers are learning to use the bathroom by themselves, ask their parents to dress them in easy-to-remove clothing. This will help prevent accidents.

Shoes and Socks

650 Put shoes and socks on active toddlers while they are sitting in highchairs.

Music

Introduction to Music

651 Give babies an introduction to music by singing lullabies and other songs to them. Or let them listen to instrumental recordings. It's never too early to begin musical training.

I've Got Rhythm

652 Babies can begin to develop a sense of rhythm through body movement. Play music with a beat and then dance your baby around in your arms, bounce him or her on your knee, or rock or pat your baby in time to the music.

Snacks

Teething Snacks

653 Frozen peas or blueberries make soothing snacks for teething children.

Baby Bottle Organizer

654 Organize baby bottles for storing in a refrigerator by placing them in a cardboard soft-drink carrier. The bottles won't tip over, and they'll be easy to tote back and forth.

Reducing Yogurt Mess

655 Are you tired of cleaning yogurt-covered tables and chairs after snack time? If so, try freezing yogurt in an ice-cube tray. Take the frozen cubes out and slice them into pieces. Toddlers love this fun finger food, and you'll love the reduced yogurt mess.

Pizza Cutter Magic

656 Use a wheeled pizza cutter to cut French toast, waffles, cheese sandwiches, etc., into small pieces for toddlers. The pizza cutter is easier and less messy to use than a knife.

Frozen Food

657 Make your own baby food by pureeing appropriate leftovers. Freeze the foods in ice-cube trays and defrost as needed.

Finger Foods

658 To encourage tiny tots to eat with their fingers, cut meats, vegetables, cheese and bread into julienne strips before serving.

Toddler Drinking Cup

659 A drinking cup will be easier for a toddler to hold if you wrap a rubber band around the outside of it.

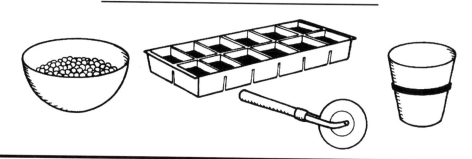

Bib Holder

660 Paint two spring-type clothespins and decorate them to look like alligators. Fasten the ends of a shoelace to the alligator tails. Clip the mouths of the alligators to a napkin to make a bib.

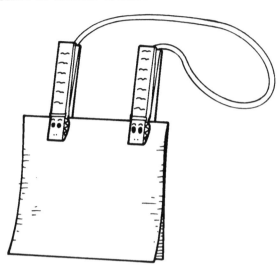

Toddler Placemats

661 Use washcloths or hand towels for toddlers' placemats. They absorb spills and are handy for wiping sticky fingers. Washcloths also make great napkins.

More Tiny Tot Tips

Entertaining Baby

662 A simple way to entertain a baby is to place a small ice cube on his or her highchair tray.

Plastic Card Mailing Game

663 Toddlers love this game. Collect old, hard-plastic membership cards such as outdated library cards or health insurance cards. Cut a slit in the plastic lid of an empty coffee can. Let your children have fun "mailing" the plastic cards through the slit.

It Takes Two

664 When you are doing tasks around a toddler, such as brushing your hair or stirring cooking ingredients, give a brush or a spoon to the child so that he or she can pretend to copy what you are doing. In this way, a fun game becomes a real learning experience.

SPECIAL TIMES TIPS

Birthday Tips

Birthday Cakes

Chalkboard Cake

665 Draw a birthday cake topped with the appropriate number of candles on a chalkboard. After singing "Happy Birthday," let the birthday child erase the candles as everyone counts.

Box Cake

666 Decorate a sturdy box with a lid to look like a birthday cake. Insert candle holders in the top of the lid. Whenever a child has a birthday, bring out the box cake and put the appropriate number of candles in the holders. (The candles are not to be lighted.) If desired, place small, giftwrapped items inside the box cake and let the birthday child reach in and choose one.

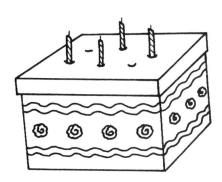

Candle Holders

667 For edible candle holders on a birthday cake, try using gumdrops or miniature marshmallows.

Celebration Tips

Birthday Flag

668 Make a birthday flag to hang in the room whenever one of your children has a birthday. Look for birthday flag patterns at large fabric stores.

Birthday Shirts

669 To honor the birthday child, let the other children use fabric paints to decorate a T-shirt for the child to wear. Inexpensive shirts can be found at discount stores or garage sales.

Starting a Tradition

670 Start a birthday tradition of letting the birthday child sit on your lap while the rest of the group sings "Happy Birthday."

Big Day Treat

671 Let the birthday child bring in a special guest on his or her big day.

Musical Celebration

672 Let your children honor the birthday child with a musical salute. Have them sing "Happy Birthday" while playing homemade rhythm instruments such as drums and maracas.

Party Pointers

How Many to Invite?

673 When planning a birthday party, a general rule of thumb is to invite no more children than the age of the birthday child.

Waiting Times

674 Be prepared to entertain those who arrive at the party first or those who must wait to be picked up when the party is over. Provide some activity such as decorating a sack for taking party favors home.

No-Lose Games

675 Make sure that the party will be fun for all ages. Plan games or activities in which everyone can participate and be a winner.

Planning Activities

676 Always have a few extra party games or activities to fall back on in case the children finish or tire quickly with what you have planned.

Party Food

677 When it comes to party food, the simpler the better. It's best to prepare most of the food ahead of time, if possible.

Party Favors

678 Losing favors can spoil an otherwise enjoyable party experience for young children. Provide each child with a bag for holding party favors and have extras on hand in case of accidents.

Summer Birthdays

All-Day Celebration

679 Honor your children who have summer birthdays by having one big celebration at the end of the school year. Pick a day during the last week your group meets and let the children participate in birthday activities all day long.

Half-Birthdays

680 Let your children who have summer birthdays celebrate their half-birthdays. Do the same kinds of activities you do for ordinary birthday celebrations. Young children especially enjoy adding "½" to their ages.

V.I.P. Day

681 When a birthday cannot be celebrated, have a V.I.P. (Very Important Person) Day for the child. Honor the child on his or her day by doing special activities.

Circle Time Tips

Seat Mats

Paper Circles

682 Place large, colorful paper circles on the floor for your children to sit on during group time. When you collect the circles, use them to reinforce color recognition.

Pizza Wheels

683 Make seat mats for your children by writing their names on cardboard pizza wheels. Let the children decorate their mats with felt-tip markers. Not only will the mats help with name recognition, they will allow you to seat the children where you wish.

Cushioned Seat Mats

684 For each child, cut out two 11-by-12-inch sheets of vinyl wallpaper and punch holes about 1 inch apart around the edges. Place a magazine or a folded newspaper between the wallpaper sheets to make a "cushion." Let the child use yarn to lace the sheets together. Then use a permanent felt-tip marker to write the children's names on their mats.

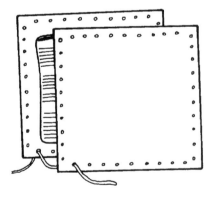 

Picture Seat Mats

685 Mount photographs of your children on large squares of posterboard. Cover the squares with clear self-stick paper and let the children use them as seat mats.

Placemats

686 Use old placemats as seat mats at circle time. Assign a different-colored or -patterned mat to each child.

Carpet Seating

687 Do your children tend to bunch up on the floor at group time? They'll give each other more space if you use masking tape to make squares on the carpet for them to sit in.

Rug Stencils

688 Define seating spaces on your carpet by using red and blue fabric paint to stencil rows of alternating rectangles (about 2 by 8 inches). This will allow you to give your children individual directions such as, "Sit only on a blue space," or "Sit on a red space in the back row."

Special Times

Special Talk Time

689 Sometime during the day, have your children join you in a close circle for a "special talk time" when you discuss socialization skills such as manners or new behavior ideas. Your children will respond well to this intimate time, and you'll find that it's very effective.

I Did a Good Job

690 Circle time provides a great opportunity to build self-esteem in your children. Have them complete the following sentence as you write down their responses: "One thing I did well today was _____." Be prepared to help any child who finds self-praise difficult.

More Circle Time Tips

Circle Time Display Board

691 Arrange to have a small display board near where your group sits at circle time. You'll find it comes in handy for posting items you wish to discuss.

Restlessness at Circle Time

692 Young children become restless if they have to sit and listen for too long. Instead of having your children name the shapes, colors or numbers of items you hold up, attach the items to a nearby wall and let your children take turns getting up and pointing to the ones you name.

Who's Turn Is It?

693 To make sure that each child gets a chance to answer a question at circle time, print name cards for all your children and put the cards into a box. Every time you need a question answered, pull a name card from the box, ask the child the question, then put the card into a can. When all the name cards are in the can, put them back into the box and start all over again. The children will wait patiently, knowing that eventually everyone will get a turn.

Changing Shape

694 Instead of circle time, have "square time" and let your children sit on the floor in the shape of a square. Later, have triangle time, rectangle time and oval time.

Cleanup Time Tips

Cleanup Signals

Quick Response

695 Give your children a consistent signal, such as a blinking light or a particular song, when it is time to clean up. Such a signal will encourage your children to respond right away.

Musical Signal

696 Select a song that has multiple verses such as "Old MacDonald Had a Farm." Tell your children that when they hear you start the song, it is time to begin cleaning up. As each child completes a cleanup task, let him or her choose a verse of the song to sing. Continue until all the children have finished.

Music Box Signal

697 As a gentle reminder to your children that it's time to clean up, turn on a music box. You will soon find many children trying to "beat Mr. Music" by finishing cleanup tasks before the music box runs down.

Cleanup Songs

Time to Clean Up

698 Make cleanup time more fun by singing the song below.

Sung to: "Frere Jacques"

Time to clean up, time to clean up
All the toys, all the toys.
Time to put the toys away,
Won't you please help me today?
Thank you, thank you.

Carol J. Luckenbill

This Is the Way

699 Sing the following song at cleanup time, substituting the name of the task at hand for *pick up the toys.*

Sung to: "The Mulberry Bush"

This is the way we pick up the toys,
Pick up the toys, pick up the toys.
This is the way we pick up the toys,
So early in the morning.

Deb Cech

Doing the Job

Mitten Dusters

700 Save mismatched mittens from your lost-and-found box. Let your children put on the mittens and use them to help you dust shelves or other room furniture.

Child-Size Equipment

701 In a convenient corner, store cleanup equipment such as small sponges, a child-size broom and mop, a whisk broom, a dustpan and a hand-held vacuum cleaner. Your children will be able to handle such equipment easily when it is time to help clean up.

Specific Tasks

702 Assign specific tasks. Instead of saying "Clean up the art area," give directions such as these: "Put the scissors in the scissors holder," or "Pick up three pieces of paper and throw them away."

A Few Minutes at a Time

703 To keep your children from becoming discouraged or bored when they are cleaning up, try scheduling several short periods of cleanup rather than one long period.

Special Responsibilities

704 At cleanup time, give each child a special responsibility. For instance, you might say, "Cody and Joseph are our kitchen cleaner-uppers today," or "Katie and Libby, please be in charge of the blocks."

Cleanup Timer

705 Use a kitchen timer to encourage your children to clean up quickly. Tell them how many minutes they have to work, then set the timer to go off when the time is up. At the sound of the bell, everyone should be finished and ready for the next activity.

Giving Positive Strokes

706 As your children are helping you clean up, be sure to give them plenty of positive reinforcement, including smiles, hugs and words of praise. Tasks will get done in no time!

Cleanup Inspector

707 To help your children take responsibility at cleanup time, choose someone each day or week to be room inspector. Have the inspector check to see that things have been put away properly and that the floor and tables are clean. This job will make your children feel important, and they'll look forward to being in charge.

Putting Things Away

Room Tour

708 At the beginning of the school year, take your children on a room tour. Show them where the toys and other materials are kept. After the children try out the different materials, show them how to put the materials away.

Picture Labels

709 Putting things away will be easier if you attach identifying pictures to the outsides of your toy containers.

Drawstring Bags

710 Make drawstring bags in several colors and let your children use them for sorting and storing toys. The colors of the bags can indicate which toys should be put inside.

Labeling Shelves

711 Label your toy shelves with different colors, shapes, numerals, etc. At cleanup time, give directions such as these: "Put the ball on the blue shelf," or "Put the toy car on the circle shelf."

Room Arrangement

712 Make cleanup time easier by keeping your room arrangement the same throughout the year. Your children will always know where things belong and will be able to put them away quickly.

Cleanup Basket

713 At cleanup time, provide a large basket with a handle. While everyone sings a cleanup song, let one child walk around the room with the basket and pick up games, toys, etc. When the basket is full, have each child take out an object and put it back where it belongs.

Cleanup Train

714 Give each of your children a basket. Let them form a "cleanup train" and walk around the room, picking things up as they go. When finished, have each child be responsible for putting away the objects in his or her basket.

Field Trip Tips

Before You Go

Plan Ahead

715 When planning to go on a field trip, call the location well in advance. Make arrangements for a guide, if necessary, and request that explanations be kept simple. Young children enjoy seeing and touching things they can identify with and understand.

Trial Run

716 Familiarize yourself with your field trip location ahead of time, if possible. Visiting the site will help you learn if there are potential hazards for young children and if water and restrooms are available.

Preparing Your Children

717 Tell your children when and where they will be going on a field trip, how they will get there, and what you expect to see. Show related photographs or pictures, if possible. Preparing your children ahead of time will relieve apprehension and make it easier for them to absorb new sights and sounds.

Chaperones

718 Organize your chaperones for a field trip ahead of time. Make sure they understand your guidelines and what is expected of them.

Transportation

719 If you are going on a field trip by car, double-check on transportation several days before you go. Be sure that you have scheduled enough vehicles and that they have the proper safety equipment for young children.

Keeping Track of One Another

Field Trip Name Tags

720 To prevent strangers from calling your children by their names, print only the name and address of your teaching center on field trip name tags. (Also make sure that your children do not wear any items with their names on them.)

Field Trip T-Shirts

721 Let your children decorate inexpensive T-shirts with fabric paint to wear when you go on field trips. Print the name and telephone number of your teaching center on the backs of the shirts.

Stamp It On

722 Before leaving on a field trip, use your teaching center's rubber address stamp and an ink pad to print the name, address and telephone number of your center on each child's hand.

Matching T-Shirts

723 To help keep track of your children on field trips, have them dress in matching T-shirts or colors.

Which Group?

724 Before you leave on a field trip, divide your children into groups and assign an adult leader to each group. Stamp the hands of the children and the adult in each group with an identical rubber stamp. This will help the children remember which group they belong to and which adult is their leader.

Here I Am!

725 If you're taking a field trip to a place where there will be lots of other people, carry a helium-filled balloon or wear a brightly colored scarf on your head so your children can spot you easily.

Jump Rope Holder

726 When going on a field trip, let your children hold onto a jump rope as they walk. This will keep them all together and help them stay in a straight line.

On the Way

Take a Break

727 Before going on a field trip, estimate the time it will take to get to the site. If it is more than half an hour, plan to take a break about halfway there.

Active Time

728 Plan an active time before your visit if the children are expected to be quiet at the site. Schedule a restroom stop before arriving.

Scenic Route

729 If possible, take a scenic route when you go on a field trip so that you can point out things of interest along the way. This will help make the travel time pass more quickly.

Watch Your Fingers

730 If you are going on a field trip by car, guard against hurt fingers by having the children put their hands on top of their heads before you close the car doors.

Things to Take

Disposable Wipes

731 For quick and easy cleanup, take along disposable wipes when going on a field trip.

Emergency Box

732 For minor emergencies on field trips, take along a box containing facial tissues, small bandages, rubber bands, safety pins, a small bar of soap, etc.

Camera and Tape Recorder

733 Take a camera and a tape recorder (or a video camera) with you on field trips. Assign an adult to be in charge of each one, since you may not have time to record as well as supervise the trip. Later, use the photos and recorded tapes to review what your children experienced.

Song Tapes

734 Take tape recordings of favorite songs to play in the car when going on field trips. If your children get restless, put on a tape and encourage everyone to sing along.

Emergency Cards

735 For each child, use a separate index card to list emergency information such as the following: name, address, telephone number, name of doctor, name of relative or neighbor, list of known allergies. Place all the cards in an envelope marked "Emergencies." When you go on a field trip, the cards will be ready to take with you.

Step Up to See

736 When you go on a field trip to a post office or other place that has high counters, take along a lightweight foot stool. Your children can take turns standing on the stool to see what is going on behind the counters.

When You Arrive

Limit Your Time

737 Don't spend too much time at a field trip site. A half hour is usually long enough for young children.

Keep Things Simple

738 On a field trip location, don't confuse your children by calling attention to every new thing in sight. Instead, help them concentrate on three or four things that are of interest.

Pointing Things Out

739 When you are pointing out something to a child on a field trip, kneel down so that you are at his or her level. This will allow you to help the child better understand what he or she is observing.

When You Return

Field Trip Display

740 When you get back from a field trip, display pictures and souvenirs of the trip to use for discussion and review. This will help keep the fun of the trip alive.

Dramatic Play

741 Set up play situations that encourage your children to reenact field trips that you take. You'll find that children enjoy using the information they learn.

Field Trip Game

742 Shortly after you return from a field trip, play a game to review the experience. Seat your children in a circle and let each one in turn complete this sentence: "I saw a _____." Continue playing as long as interest lasts.

Field Trip Book

743 A field trip experience does not have to end as soon as you return. Let your children dictate sentences about what they did on their trip while you write down each response on a separate piece of paper. After the children have illustrated their sentences, fasten their papers together to make a book for your reading corner.

Thank-You Card

744 After a field trip, make a thank-you card in an appropriate shape (a toothbrush shape for a trip to a dentist's office, a pumpkin shape for a visit to a pumpkin farm, etc.). If your children are unable to sign their own names, let them each make an inked fingerprint on the card. Then write each child's name under his or her fingerprint.

Holiday Tips

Christmas

Artificial Snow

745 Make artificial snow by whipping Ivory Snow soap powder with water until it is the consistency of cake frosting. Apply the "snow" to windows or evergreen branches.

Lighted Windows

746 To hang Christmas tree lights on your windows, use small, clear-plastic suction cups with hooks.

Decorating Your Tree

747 Put up a small tree the first week of December. As your children make ornaments over the next few weeks, hang the ornaments on your tree. When it's time for your Christmas party, your tree will be completely decorated.

Limiting Activities

748 Make sure you do not go overboard with holiday preparations. Too many exciting activities before Christmas can overshadow the day itself, making it seem dull by comparison.

Catalog Shopping

749 Save Christmas catalogs you get in the mail and let your children use them to "shop" for Christmas presents.

Christmas Shopping Games

750 Some stores provide colorful paper shopping bags during the Christmas season. Make a collection of bags and let your children use them for playing Christmas-shopping games.

Sharing the Holidays

751 Let your children share the holidays with others by making greeting cards for the residents of a retirement home, going caroling, or helping to clean up a vacant lot or a small section of a park. Doing such activities will help the children begin to understand the true meaning of Christmas.

Christmas Cards

752 Let your children make and send Christmas cards as a way of saying thank you to neighborhood helpers such as mail carriers, police officers and firefighters.

Easter

Basic Egg Dye

753 Use this recipe to dye hard-boiled eggs. In a cup or small bowl, mix together ½ cup boiling water, 1 teaspoon vinegar and about ½ teaspoon food coloring. Dip one egg at a time into the mixture.

Tissue-Paper Dye

754 Cover hard-boiled eggs with scraps of colored tissue paper and moisten them with water. As the paper adheres to the eggs, it will transfer some of its dye to the shells. Allow the tissue scraps to dry and fall off naturally.

Crepe-Paper Dye

755 Dye hard-boiled eggs with scraps of crepe paper by following the directions above for dyeing with tissue paper.

Yellow Eggs

756 For yellow eggs, first boil yellow onion skins in water for about 20 minutes, then allow the mixture to cool in the pan. After removing the onion skins, use the liquid to hard-boil eggs.

Brown Eggs

757 To make brown eggs, boil four tea bags in water. Then hard-boil eggs in the extra-strong tea.

Pink Eggs

758 As you are hard-boiling eggs, add several cups of canned beet juice and 1 to 2 tablespoons vinegar to the water. Let your pink eggs cool in the liquid, in the refrigerator, for about an hour.

Purple Eggs

759 For lavender eggs, follow the above directions for making pink eggs, substituting grape juice for beet juice.

Blue Eggs

760 To make blue hard-boiled eggs, toss a few handfuls of shredded purple cabbage into the water. Add a splash of vinegar. When cooked, allow the eggs to cool in the liquid, in the refrigerator, for at least an hour.

Crisscross Egg Designs

761 Wrap a hard-boiled egg with rubber bands before dipping it into dye. Remove the bands to reveal crisscross designs.

Multicolored Egg Designs

762 Dip a hard-boiled egg partway into several different dyes to create a multicolored layered look.

Crayon Egg Designs

763 Use a white crayon to draw a design or write a name on a hard-boiled egg. Dip the egg into dye to reveal the design.

Small Leaf Egg Designs

764 Place small leaves or fern fronds around a hard-boiled egg and wrap the egg in a square cut from a nylon stocking. Secure the nylon with a long piece of string that you hold on to when dipping the egg into dye. Later, remove the nylon square and the leaves to reveal delicate nature patterns.

Egg-Drying Rack

765 When dyeing eggs, turn an empty egg carton upside down for an instant drying rack.

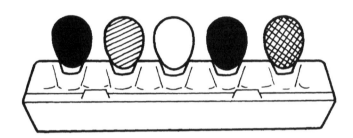

Year-Round Egg Fun

766 Extend Easter fun by dyeing eggs any time of year, especially when an activity is needed for a rainy day. Use the eggs for snacks or lunches.

Blown Eggs

767 With a pin, poke a small hole through the small end of an uncooked egg that has been brought to room temperature. Poke a larger hole (about ¼ inch in diameter) through the large end of the egg, puncturing the yolk, if possible. Blow through the small hole to force the egg yolk and white out the large hole. Then rinse out the eggshell and let it dry.

Blown Egg Handles

768 Thread yarn through a long needle and tie a large knot in the end. Poke the needle through the large hole in a blown egg and out the small hole. The knot should hold inside the shell, allowing the yarn coming out of the small hole to be used as a handle when decorating the egg.

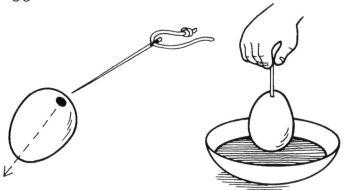

Blown Egg Alternative

769 Make a pinhole in the small end of an uncooked egg and a hole about the size of a dime in the large end. Then shake the egg yolk and white out the larger hole. After the shell has been rinsed, dried and decorated, cover the larger hole with a decorative sticker.

No-Lose Easter Egg Hunt 1

770 Often during an Easter egg hunt, a few children find many eggs while others find hardly any. To prevent this, write your children's names on the eggs.

No-Lose Easter Egg Hunt 2

771 Here's another way to have a successful Easter egg hunt. Show your children three or four different colors of eggs. Then say that everyone may search for one egg of each color to keep.

Living Easter Baskets

772 Make an Easter basket that's alive! Cut a four-cup section from a plastic-foam egg carton and attach a pipe cleaner for a handle. Spoon potting soil into the egg cups and let your children sprinkle on grass seeds. Water regularly and in about 10 days the basket will be filled with real "Easter grass."

Easter Basket Treats

773 Instead of filling Easter baskets with candy eggs and other sweets, use treats such as raisins, nuts, sugarless gum, popcorn, fruit leather, stickers, balloons, playdough, crayons, sidewalk chalk, plastic animals, blocks, rubber balls, bubble bath and bathtub toys.

Gifts and Cards

Personalized Gifts

774 Whenever your children make personalized gifts, such as clay handprint plaques or ornaments decorated with their photographs, be sure to label the gifts with the date as well as the children's names. Knowing how old the children were when they made the gifts will be especially important in later years.

Gifts of Time

775 Here's a special gift idea to use for holiday times. Let your children draw or cut out pictures that show tasks they can do at home such as picking up toys or raking leaves. Have the children glue the pictures on paper and give them to their parents as promises to do those tasks.

Cards for Everyone

776 Be aware of different family situations when your children are making greeting cards. For instance, having children with stepparents make two Mother's Day or Father's Day cards can prevent confusion or hurt feelings.

Halloween

No-Tip Jack-O'-Lantern

777 Here's a way to make a jack-o'-lantern that is easy to light and hard to tip over. Cut a section off the bottom of a pumpkin rather than the top. Scoop out the seeds and carve the pumpkin as usual. Place a votive candle on a baking sheet, light it, then put your jack-o'-lantern over the candle.

Reusable Pumpkins

778 During the Halloween season, place two large pumpkins on newspapers in your art corner for the children to paint. At the end of each day, wash the pumpkins in sudsy water, allow them to dry, and they will be ready for two more children to paint the next day.

Stone Pumpkins

779 If pumpkins are not available for Halloween, try this. Let your children paint large, smooth stones orange and then glue on green construction paper stems.

Sleeper Costumes

780 Old blanket sleepers that children can still wear can be decorated to make Halloween costumes such as bunny suits or clown outfits. Because other clothing can be worn underneath the sleepers, the costumes will be warm and comfortable.

Face Paint

781 Make face paint by mixing 2 tablespoons white vegetable shortening with 2 tablespoons cornstarch. Add drops of food coloring as desired. This face paint wipes off easily and is nontoxic.

Eye Masks

782 Here's an easy way to make eye masks for your children to wear. For each mask, cut two adjoining egg cups out of a cardboard egg carton and make eye holes in the bottoms of the cups. Let the children decorate the masks as desired. Then attach pipe cleaners to the sides of the masks and bend them to fit over the children's ears.

Trick-Or-Treat Goodies

783 Instead of candy at Halloween, give your children treats such as sugarless gum, stickers, colored pencils or fancy erasers.

Jack-O'-Lantern Oranges

784 For a fun Halloween snack, use a permanent felt-tip marker to draw jack-o'-lantern faces on oranges.

Halloween Orange Juice

785 Use black self-stick paper or plastic tape to make jack-o'-lantern faces on the sides of clear-plastic cups. Then fill the cups with orange juice for a fun Halloween treat.

Quiet Times

Holiday Seating

786 Just before a holiday, try this idea to assure a quiet time for listening to a story or singing a song. Attach masking tape to the floor in a large holiday shape, such as a Christmas tree, a heart or an egg. Make X's on the shape to indicate where each "holiday decoration" is to sit.

No Noisy Toys

787 Guard against overstimulation during holiday times by eliminating noisy toys from your children's environment.

Quiet-Time Activities

788 Plan lots of quiet-time activities for your children during holiday times. Too much holiday activity at school can overshadow the holidays at home.

Holiday Stories

789 Here's an idea for a quiet holiday activity. Tape-record favorite holiday stories word for word so that your children can listen to them while following along in the books.

Recycling Holiday Materials

Greeting Card Lotto

790 Collect nine different pairs of holiday greeting cards with matching pictures on the fronts. Use one set of the pictures to make a game board and the other set to make game cards. To play, your children can place the game cards on top of the matching pictures on the game board.

Greeting Card Ornaments

791 Cut pictures out of the fronts of old holiday greeting cards and let your children decorate them with glitter. For hangers, tie on loops of yarn or ribbon.

Wrapping Paper Pictures

792 Cut matching shapes from several kinds of used holiday wrapping paper. Glue the shapes on separate index cards to use for matching and sorting games.

Holiday Card Wreath

793 Cut out and discard the centers of paper plates. Let your children glue pictures from old holiday greeting cards on the plate rims to make wreaths. Add bows before hanging.

Cardboard Tube Fort

794 Save the cardboard tubes from rolls of wrapping paper. Let your children tape the tubes together to make a fort or other structure.

Ribbon Tubes

795 Collect empty plastic ribbon tubes and let your children use them for sorting, stacking and rolling.

Wrapping Paper Art

796 Store scraps of wrapping paper from different holidays in separate envelopes or boxes. Your children can use the scraps for collages or other art projects during holiday times.

Holiday Lacing Cards

797 Save the fronts of old greeting cards. Punch holes around the edges of the cards and let your children lace yarn through the holes.

Valentine's Day

Mail From Loveland

798 After your children make valentines for their families, put their cards in addressed, stamped envelopes. Then place all the cards in one large envelope and mail it to Postmaster, Loveland, CO 80537. If your valentines arrive in Loveland by February 6, they will be mailed again with a Loveland postmark and arrive in time for Valentine's Day.

Valentine Candy Boxes

799 Around Valentine's Day, use heart-shaped candy boxes to hold the pieces of individual puzzles or games. After the holiday, keep the boxes to use again the following year.

Wrapping Paper

Tablecloth Giftwrap

800 For a different kind of giftwrap, cut a paper holiday tablecloth into large squares.

Homemade Wrapping Paper

801 Let your children make their own holiday giftwrap. Have them print designs on butcher paper or plain newsprint with cookie cutters or holiday sponge shapes dipped into paint.

Road Map Giftwrap

802 Keep old or outdated road maps. Let your children use them as unusual holiday wrapping paper for presents they make.

Newspaper Giftwrap

803 Old newspapers are great to use for wrapping presents. Just add colored yarn or ribbon. Or let your children print holiday designs on the newspapers, if desired.

Wallpaper Giftwrap

804 Use leftover pieces of wallpaper or wallpaper samples for wrapping presents. Choose colors that are appropriate for the holiday.

Fabric Giftwrap

805 Save odds and ends of fabric pieces to use for holiday giftwrap. Tie with colorful rickrack or yarn.

More Holiday Tips

Gift Bags

806 Let your children stencil holiday designs on plain paper lunch bags. Punch two holes in the tops of each bag and insert yarn or ribbon for ties.

Supermarket Decorations

807 Supermarkets often put up decorations for holidays. Ask a local store to donate decorations after taking them down.

Holiday Hats

808 Purchase a supply of white paper hats (the kind worn by restaurant workers) through a restaurant-supply store or a local restaurant. Throughout the year, let your children decorate the hats for different holidays and wear them in marching band parades.

Holiday Confetti Shaker

809 Cut three ½-inch holes in the lid of an empty yogurt container. Fill the container with paper confetti in holiday colors and give it a shake, shake, shake!

Seasonal Card Game

810 Collect five or six greeting cards each from different holidays throughout the year. Cut the fronts off the cards and store them in an envelope. Let your children sort the cards by season.

Holiday Drinking Straws

811 For a festive touch, stick drinking straws through appropriate paper shapes at holiday times. Use pumpkin shapes for Halloween, heart shapes for Valentine's Day, etc.

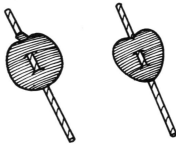

Holiday Snacks

812 For fun holiday snacks, use cookie cutters to cut bread slices into holiday shapes. The bread can be used to make sandwiches or toast.

Outdoor Time Tips

Blowing Bubbles

Straw Bubble Blowers

813 Straws are great to use for blowing bubbles. To prevent your children from accidentally sucking up the soapy water, poke a hole near the top of each straw.

Safe Bubbles

814 Use baby shampoo to make safe bubbles for bubble blowing.

Longer Lasting Bubbles

815 Make bubbles last longer by adding a few tablespoons of sugar to your soapy water.

More Longer Lasting Bubbles

816 Another trick for making longer-lasting bubbles is to let your bubble mixture stand for a day or two before using it.

Bubble Recipe 1

817 Mix together 2 quarts water, ¼ cup glycerin and ¾ cup liquid dishwashing detergent. Let your children use the mixture for blowing bubbles.

Bubble Recipe 2

818 For a fun bubble mixture, combine 10 cups water, 1 cup Joy dishwashing liquid and ¼ cup light corn syrup.

Bubble Mixture Measuring Jug

819 Making a bubble mixture is quick and easy with a measuring jug like this one. Start with an empty gallon milk jug. After adding each ingredient in a bubble recipe, make a mark on the outside of the jug to indicate the liquid level. Also write the name of the ingredient just added. When the jug is empty, you can simply pour in new ingredients up to the marked liquid levels without having to measure them out separately.

Outdoor Clothing

No More Lost Mittens

820 To cut down on the number of lost mittens, try safety-pinning or clipping them to the cuffs of your children's jackets.

Keeping Hands Dry

821 Put disposable plastic gloves over your children's knit gloves to keep their hands dry in snowy weather.

Labeling Outdoor Clothing

822 Ask parents to put their children's names in coats and jackets. This will make dressing for outdoors easier, especially if your children have similar-looking items of clothing.

A New Idea for Old Leg Warmers

823 When dressing children for snow play, slip old leg warmers over their arms after putting on their snowsuits and mittens. The leg warmers will prevent snow from getting between their mittens and their sleeves, keeping wrists warm and toasty.

Stuck Zippers

824 If zippers stick, don't despair! Rub them with a lead pencil to get them gliding smoothly again.

Pulling on Boots

825 When boots don't seem to want to go on over a child's shoes, put plastic bags over his or her shoes first. The boots should slip on easily.

Make 'Em Stay Put

826 Prevent knitted hats and mittens from falling on the floor or getting lost. Glue strips of Velcro to cubbies for your children to put their hats and mittens on.

Outdoor Play

Outdoor Seat Mats

827 Cut plastic shower curtains into squares and let your children use them for outdoor seat mats.

Colored Wrist Bands

828 Before playing outdoor games or relays, avoid the mix-up that can occur when children forget their team numbers. Have your children wear different colors of elastic around their wrists to signify the different teams.

Sunny Day House Painting

829 On a sunny day, let your children "paint" outside walls, fences and other surfaces with water and large paintbrushes.

Little Squirts

830 Fill clean squirt bottles with water. When the weather is hot, let your children take the bottles outside to use for water play.

Car Wash

831 For a fun project that's practical too, assemble your outdoor riding toys and let the children have a "car wash."

Toddler Snow Shovel

832 Give a toddler a dustpan to use for a snow shovel. It's just the right height and size.

Snow Toys

833 Plastic containers, such as margarine tubs, are great to use for snow play. Encourage your children to pack the containers with snow and then tap out the molded shapes.

Cold Weather Protection

834 A coating of petroleum jelly will protect children's cheeks when they are playing outdoors in cold or windy weather.

Ending Outdoor Time

835 When it's time to stop playing and come indoors, these two signals will help get your children's attention. First, raise one hand as a signal to line up. Then, with the children who are first to form a line, start counting together or saying the alphabet. When the others hear this second signal, they will quickly join in line to help with the counting or naming.

Picnics

Picnic Pails

836 When you're going to a play area for a picnic and don't want to take along extra toys, try this. Use peanut butter pails with handles to carry your lunches. After eating, your children can use the pails with plastic spoons for sandbox play.

Picnic Trash Bag

837 Here's a way to make a picnic trash bag that will stand up by itself but won't leak. Simply place a plastic bag inside a brown paper grocery bag and fold the top down several times. Throw away your trash bag when it becomes full.

Washcloth Wiper

838 Place a wet, soapy washcloth in a travel soap-bar case to take with you when you go on a picnic. Use the cloth for wiping off sticky hands.

Playground Tips

Non-Slip Swing Seats 1

839 If swing seats are too slippery, cover them with a coat of paint mixed with some fine sand. The sand will provide just enough traction, and it won't scratch.

Non-Slip Swing Seats 2

840 Cover slippery swing seats with pieces of foam rubber to add traction.

Non-Slip Swing Seats 3

841 Solve the problem of slippery swing seats by gluing on non-slip strips that are sold for use in bathtubs.

Fixing a Sticky Slide

842 To slick up a sticky slide, have your children take turns going down it while sitting on sheets of waxed paper. Repeat the process as many times as necessary, handing out fresh pieces of waxed paper as needed.

Keep It Cool

843 Prevent burns by placing your metal slide out of direct sunlight.

Cushioning Falls

844 Falls are the most common form of playground accident. Provide a cushion by covering your playground with a material such as sand or wood chips.

Giant Sandbox

845 Place a tractor tire flat on the ground. Fill the round hole in the center with sand to make a sandbox that can be used by several children at a time.

Outdoor Soap Sock

846 Save slivers of soap in an old nylon stocking. Tie the stocking on an outdoor faucet for your children to use when washing their hands.

Keep Our Playground Clean

847 Place a covered trash can on your playground so that any litter can be disposed of immediately. Your children will be more likely to use the can if it's right there when needed.

Walks and Nature Hikes

Walking Train

848 To discourage stragglers when taking a walk, try this. Make a "train" by stringing large wooden beads on a length of clothesline, spacing them apart, and knotting the rope before and after each bead. Your children can each hold onto a bead and take turns being the "engine" and the "caboose."

Nature Walk Bag

849 When you take your children on a nature walk, carry a shopping bag for holding items you find along the way. An open shoe box placed in the bottom will make the bag sturdier.

Magnifying Glass Fun

850 Take along a magnifying glass when you go on walks so your children can observe nature up close.

Preserving Nature Items

851 On nature walks, carry a bottle of hairspray for spritzing delicate weeds and fluffy seed pods that your children collect. This will help preserve the fragile items. (Stand away from children when using hairspray.)

Treasure Boxes

852 When going on nature walks, give each of your children an empty egg carton in which to put found treasures. Later, the items can be glued in the cartons, if desired.

Nature Walk Bracelets

853 Before going on a nature walk, put a band of masking tape, sticky side out, around each child's wrist. The "bracelets" can be used for holding leaves, seeds and other small, lightweight items that the children collect.

Mini-Nature Walk

854 If there is no place close by for a nature walk, try this. Let your children form circles on a grassy area with pieces of string. Give them each a magnifying glass and let them explore the grass inside their circles to see what tiny nature items they can discover.

Cereal Necklaces

855 Wearable snacks are great for walks and nature hikes. Thread *O*-shaped cereal pieces on lengths of string to make edible necklaces.

Apple Necklaces

856 Core apples and string them on loops of ribbon. Your children will love wearing these edible necklaces on walks or hikes.

Frozen Grapes

857 Before going on a walk with your children, freeze red or green seedless grapes to take along. They taste great on a hot day!

Magic Wands

858 Stick black olives on the ends of pretzel sticks. The "magic wands" make a great snack for taking on a walk.

Show and Tell Tips

Scheduling

Be Consistent

859 Choose a specific day for Show and Tell and consistently schedule the activity each week. Mondays are generally poor choices because children tend to forget about the activity over the weekend.

Setting Limits

860 Sharing time will go more smoothly if you limit the number of children who share each day. Listeners will be more attentive and polite. And the children will take greater care in deciding what to bring for sharing on their special days.

Show and Tell Plan

861 To avoid a long, drawn-out Show and Tell time, designate one day each week as sharing day. Divide your children into four or five groups and assign one sharing day a month to each group. Then each Monday, post the names of the children who have sharing time that week.

Keeping Parents Informed

862 Keep parents informed of your Show and Tell schedule so that they can help their children prepare for the activity. This can be done by posting the information on your parent bulletin board each week.

Show and Tell Items

Display Table

863 Provide a table or a corner in your room for displaying items brought in for Show and Tell. Arrange a special time for your children to see what is on display and to listen to those who have something to share.

Show and Tell Bags

864 Young children often like to keep the items they bring in for Show and Tell a surprise. Let each child make a Show and Tell bag by decorating a heavy paper sack or a cloth bag made out of old sheeting material. Label the bags with the children's names and add handles for easy toting.

Drawstring Sharing Bag

865 Make a special drawstring bag to use for sharing time. Write "Show and Tell" and your teaching center's name on the bag. Let your children take turns using the bag to bring in treasures for Show and Tell on their sharing days.

Special Sharing Days

Show and Tell Variations

866 Instead of always having traditional Show and Tell time, try scheduling special sharing days now and then. Choose a theme for each day and have everyone bring in a related item to share. Be sure to let parents know about these special days well ahead of time.

Color Day

867 Have your children bring in Show and Tell items that are a particular color such as red or yellow. Give everyone a chance to share his or her treasure.

Signs of the Season Day

868 Celebrate a new season by having your children bring in appropriate items to share, such as colored leaves for fall or blossoming branches for spring.

Song Day

869 Let each child in turn share a favorite song by singing it for the group. Give help with words or tunes as needed.

Bathtub Day

870 For a special sharing day, have your children bring in items they use in the bathtub. They will talk about everything from a packaged soap bar to a rubber duckie!

Baby Picture Day

871 Have your children bring in baby pictures of themselves to share with the group. Ask them to tell about such things as their eye and hair color at birth and how much they weighed.

Book Day

872 Ask each child to bring in a favorite book to share. Let the child tell one or two sentences about the book while showing the group several of the illustrations.

Flower Day

873 Have each child bring in a favorite flower, either fresh or dried. After sharing the flowers with the group, have your children place them in a vase to make a "sharing bouquet."

Snack Time Tips

Food Tips

Sandwich Leftovers

874 When you make sandwiches by cutting matching shapes out of bread, cheese and lunch-meat slices, save all the leftover scraps. Make stuffing or croutons with the bread pieces and use the cheese and meat scraps as pizza or cracker toppings.

Vegetable Leftovers

875 Save leftover vegetables, such as carrots, potatoes, peas and green beans, from snack time. Store them separately in a freezer to use when you make a pot of soup with your children. (Beets, green peppers, eggplant, leafy greens, cabbage, broccoli and Brussels sprouts are not recommended as soup vegetables.)

Cereal Crumbs

876 Crumble leftover dry cereal. Keep the crumbs in an airtight container to use as a crunchy topping for yogurt, applesauce or casseroles.

Hard Cheese

877 Don't throw out cheese that has become too hard to slice. Instead, let your children help grate it for pizza toppings.

Soggy Crackers

878 Crackers that have lost their crunch can be revitalized by placing them in a hot oven for a minute or two.

Thin Soup

879 Thicken watery soup in a minute by stirring in a small amount of instant potato flakes.

Unripe Fruit

880 Hard fruit will ripen more quickly if you place it in a brown paper grocery bag.

Keeping Apples White

881 Here's an easy way to prevent apple slices from turning brown. Immediately after the slices have been cut, sprinkle them with lemon juice.

Ripe Bananas

882 Bananas ripen quickly if left out on a counter top. To stop the ripening process, place them in a refrigerator.

Storing Fresh Vegetables

883 Fresh vegetables will last longer in your refrigerator if you first wrap them in damp paper towels and then place them in plastic bags.

Tasty Tomatoes

884 If you want tomatoes to retain their flavor, do not store them in a refrigerator. Use them right away or keep them out on a kitchen counter for a few days.

Crisping Carrot Sticks

885 Bring limp carrot sticks back to life by soaking them for about an hour in ice water. Add a splash of lemon juice, then drain the carrots. Put them into a plastic bag and store them in a refrigerator. Try this method for crisping celery sticks too.

Learning With Snacks

Learning Colors

886 When you are working on a particular color, such as red, serve red food (apples, tomatoes, red bell peppers, etc.) at snack time. Use matching-colored placemats and napkins, if desired.

Colored Milk

887 Reinforce color concepts by adding a few drops of food coloring to milk served at snack time. This may also encourage children who don't like milk to drink it.

Colored Topping

888 For a tasty way to review colors, add small amounts of dry, flavored, sugar-free gelatin to whipped topping or whipped cream. Choose lemon flavor for yellow, cherry flavor for red, and so on.

Learning Shapes

889 Serve different-shaped crackers to review shapes. Cut cheese slices into matching shapes to place on top, if desired.

Cookies in Geometric Shapes

890 After rolling out cookie dough, use a pastry wheel to cut out squares, rectangles, diamonds and triangles. Then use the rim of a drinking glass to cut out circles. Bake the cookies according to your recipe directions.

Learning Numbers

891 To review numbers, let your children count how many raisins, carrot sticks, pretzels, etc., they will eat for a snack each day.

Clip and Count

892 Here's a fun way to review numbers at snack time. Place a small dowel upright in a lump of playdough (or other kind of holder) on your snack table. Set out crackers or other food items. Clip spring-type clothespins to the side of the dowel to indicate how many crackers each child may place on his or her plate. Encourage your children to count the clothespins, then count out their crackers.

Pouring and Passing

Dry Run

893 Before letting your children pour liquids from a pitcher, have them practice pouring dry ingredients such as rice or salt.

Pouring Pitcher

894 A see-through pitcher made of clear plastic or glass makes it easier for young children to control portions when they are pouring milk or juice.

Measuring Cup Pitcher

895 Let your children use a plastic measuring cup for a pouring pitcher.

Catching Spills

896 An open dishwasher door makes a perfect "table" for pouring liquids. Just close the door and spills will be gone.

Baby Bottle Measuring Cup

897 Use a clear-plastic baby bottle to make an easy-to-hold measuring cup for your children. Remove the top, saving it to use on other bottles, if desired. Then use a permanent felt-tip marker to add black lines and numbers to the outside of the bottle.

Muffin Tin Trays

898 Let your children use muffin tins as trays when passing out cups of milk or juice. The muffin tins will help keep the cups from tipping over.

Snack Time Caddy

899 A well-scrubbed plastic caddy (the kind used for holding household cleaning supplies) is great for carrying cups, napkins, bottles of juice, etc., to the table at snack time.

Snack Time Trays

900 Instead of giving your children handfuls of utensils to pass out at snack time, let them use trays. Line the trays with colorful paper and lay out spoons, forks, etc., on top. Your children will find the trays easy to hold when going around the table.

Lightweight Trays

901 Make lightweight trays by cutting rectangles out of plastic-foam board and covering them with colored or patterned self-stick paper. Your children can use the trays to carry nonbreakable items such as napkins or paper cups.

Preparing Snacks

Involving Your Children

902 When doing cooking activities, choose recipes that allow your children to participate in the preparation. For instance, make soups that involve washing and peeling vegetables or breads that involve measuring, stirring and kneading.

Stove-Top Cooking

903 When cooking on a stove top, use the back burners whenever possible and keep all pot handles turned to the back, out of the children's reach.

Get Out the Grinder

904 A baby food grinder is a great appliance to have for preparing snacks. Use it for making tuna salad or egg salad, mashing bananas, grinding nuts, grating cheeses, grinding dried fruits, mashing potatoes and softening butter or margarine.

Peeling Vegetables

905 Using vegetable peelers can be hazardous for little fingers. Instead, let your children use spoons to scrape off the outer skins of carrots and similar vegetables.

Snack and Share

906 When making a quick bread, such as banana bread, double the recipe and bake one half of the batter in a loaf pan and the other half in small metal juice cans. Your children can enjoy the large loaf at snack time and take the small loaves home as gifts.

Whose Muffin Is It?

907 Try this idea for keeping track of your children's muffin creations. Trace around the outside of the muffin tin on a piece of paper and draw circles to indicate the individual cups. As each child fills a muffin-tin cup with batter, write that child's name in the corresponding circle on the paper. Be sure to mark the top of your drawing and the muffin tin.

Surprise Messages

908 When you are baking muffins or cupcakes, wrap little notes in aluminum foil and place them in the batter. Your children will love breaking open their treats to find the surprise messages.

Cutting Made Easy

909 Partially freeze bread slices before you cut shapes out of them with cookie cutters. The cutting will be much easier.

Spreadable Peanut Butter

910 Blend peanut butter with mashed bananas, pureed peaches, applesauce or apple-juice concentrate. This soft, easy-to-spread mixture will help prevent torn bread slices.

Molded Gelatin Shapes

911 When making molded gelatin shapes for special occasions, add a teaspoon of white vinegar to the gelatin and water mixture. The shapes will hold up better when you take them out of the molds.

Frosting Cookies

912 Young children enjoy frosting their own cookies or muffins. To make the job easier and more fun, put the frosting into mustard or catsup squeeze bottles that have been thoroughly washed and dried.

Easy Graham Cracker Crumbs

913 Here's a quick way to make graham cracker crumbs. Place the crackers inside a clear-plastic bag and close the top. Then lay the bag out flat and roll a large drinking glass or a rolling pin over it. Continue until the crumbs are the desired size.

Serving Sizes

914 The rule of thumb for a child's serving size of meats, vegetables and fruits is 1 tablespoon per year of age.

Kitchen Coveralls

915 When your children are helping prepare snacks, give them old adult-size T-shirts to wear. The large shirts will cover their clothes and are easy to wash. If the sleeves are too baggy, slip elastic into the sleeve hems.

Snack Ideas

No-Bake Cookies

916 Purchase large, soft cookies. Use a small cookie cutter to cut a shape out of each cookie. Then let your children decorate the cookie shapes with frosting. (Save the leftovers to use for dessert toppings.)

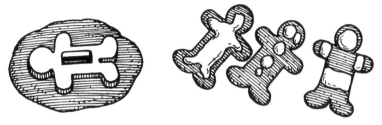

Paintbrush Cookies

917 Here's a fun way to decorate cookies without using frosting. Combine 1 egg yolk with ¼ teaspoon water and mix thoroughly. Divide the mixture into small cups and add drops of food coloring. Let your children use new small brushes to paint the mixture on unbaked cookies. Then bake the cookies according to your recipe directions. If the "paint" thickens, add a few drops of water.

Easy Cake Decoration

918 When you don't want to frost a cake, try this. Place a paper doily on top of the cake and sift on powdered sugar or powdered cocoa. Gently remove the doily to reveal a lacy design.

Yogurt Cheese

919 Try making this great-tasting, nonfat alternative to cream cheese. Place plain nonfat yogurt in cheesecloth. Put the cheesecloth into a strainer and the strainer into a bowl, then refrigerate overnight. The liquid in the yogurt will drain through the cheesecloth and the yogurt will take on a smooth consistency similar to cream cheese. Serve with crackers or quick breads.

Salt Substitute

920 If your children want to "salt" their food, give them this salt substitute to shake on instead. Mix together sodium-free salt, paprika, onion powder, Parmesan cheese and very fine parsley flakes. Then pour the mixture into shaker containers.

Fruity Yogurt

921 Make fruity yogurt the easy way. Just add a small amount of all-fruit, sugarless jam to plain nonfat yogurt.

Applesauce Treat

922 For a special treat on a hot day, freeze applesauce in frozen-pop molds.

Ice-Cube Treats

923 When making ice cubes for special occasions, try this. Drop a small piece of fruit into each compartment of an ice-cube tray. Then pour in juice instead of water and freeze.

Snack Table Tips

Centerpieces

924 For special days, provide centerpieces for your snack table. Let your children share in the making of the centerpieces. Or make them yourself as a surprise from the teacher.

Place Cards

925 To help your children with name recognition and to encourage them to make new friends, make place cards for them to put on the table at snack time.

Paper Cup Place Cards

926 Write the names of your children on paper cups and use the cups as place cards.

Napkin Rings

927 Make napkin rings by cutting cardboard tubes into sections and covering them with aluminum foil or colorful wrapping paper.

My Own Placemat

928 Snack time will become special if you let each child design his or her own placemat to use on the snack table. Cover each placemat with clear self-stick paper for durability.

Washable Placemats

929 Make washable placemats out of vinyl window shades. On each mat, use a permanent felt-tip marker to draw a large circle for a plate and a small circle for a cup in their proper places. Label each mat at the top by writing "Leah's Place," "Christopher's Place," etc.

Table-Setting Placemats

930 To help your children learn how to set a table, make plastic-covered placemats with cutouts of knives, forks, spoons, cups, plates and napkins glued in their proper places.

Plastic Placemats

931 Cut clean, plastic curtains into rectangles to use as placemats on your snack table.

Photo Placemats

932 Make placemats by gluing snapshots of your children on separate posterboard rectangles. Let the children add decorations as desired. Then cover the placemats with clear self-stick paper.

Seasonal Placemats

933 Have your children decorate placemats for each season. Use a design such as a tree in spring, summer, fall and winter. All four placemats can be sent home at the end of the year.

Puzzle Placemats

934 For each child, make a different-colored or patterned placemat and cut off one of the corners. At snack time, let your children find their places by matching the corners with the corresponding placemats.

Preventing Spills

935 To prevent accidental spills at the snack table, encourage your children to put their cups of milk or juice above their plates rather than to the side.

Sitting Down for Snacks

936 Help develop good eating habits early. Instead of letting your children eat while standing or walking around, always have them sit at the table.

Tummy to the Table

937 To encourage your children to sit close to the table when eating, try using this saying: "Tummy to the table, girls and boys." The saying provides a clear picture of what the children are to do, and they'll enjoy using it as a reminder among themselves.

Floor Covering

938 Placing newspaper or plastic sheets under your snack table will help catch spills and keep the area clean.

More Snack Time Tips

Frozen Snacks

939 Frozen snacks on sticks are a real favorite, but they're messy to eat. To catch drips, poke the sticks through the centers of small paper plates.

Personal Cups

940 Here's a way to cut down on paper cup use. Have your children bring in their own cups, labeled with their names, to use for milk, juice or water at snack time. The cups should be thoroughly washed and dried each day.

Lunch Boxes

941 Cut plastic-foam egg cartons with lids in half the short way to make lunch boxes. Clean the cartons thoroughly, and place small pieces of different foods in the egg cups. Your children will love having their snacks served this way!

How Much Is Enough?

942 Parents often object when children overeat at snack time. To help your children remember how much food is enough, try this saying: "One mouth, one (glass of juice, etc.); two hands, two (crackers, etc.)."

Juice Box Straws

943 After serving juice box snacks, save and wash a few of the straws. They will come in handy if you ever have juice boxes with missing straws.

Clip Them Closed

944 After opening loaves of bread or packages of snack foods, close the bags and secure them with spring-type clothespins. The clothespins are much easier to use than twist ties.

Refrigerator Fun

945 Here's a tip for keeping your children busy while you are preparing snacks. Tape a piece of butcher paper to the door or the side of your refrigerator and let the children draw pictures on it while they are waiting for you to finish.

Transition Time Tips

Beginning of the Year

Sticker Fun

946 To ease the transition between home and school during the first few days of the year, try this. Attach a different sticker to each child's cubby. Then give each parent several matching stickers to attach, one a day, to the back of the child's hand just before coming to school. Upon arrival, the children will be eager to locate their cubbies by finding their matching stickers.

Labeling Cubbies

947 At the beginning of the school year, take an instant photo of each child, print his or her name at the bottom, and tape the picture above the child's cubby. This will make it easy for your children to locate their cubbies while they are learning to recognize their names.

Beginning the Day

Feed the Fishes

948 Saying goodbye to Mom or Dad at school can be difficult for a little one. Help ease a difficult separation by carrying the child over to your fish tank and letting him or her feed the fish. The physical contact, the water and the fish are all very soothing.

Welcoming Your Children

949 Your children will find the transition between home and school easier if you are standing at the door to greet them each morning.

Parent Helpers

950 On some mornings ask parents (who have the time) to stay for a few minutes and help welcome the children in your group. This will make the morning transition time easier.

A School of Fish

951 For each child, cut a different fish shape out of construction paper and print the child's name on it. Cover the fish shapes with clear self-stick paper and place them in a box. When your children arrive each morning, have them find their own fish shapes and pin them to a bulletin board. The "school of fish" will allow you to see at a glance which children are present that day.

Seasonal Name Tags

952 Each month cut different seasonal shapes from construction paper, label them with your children's names, then cover the shapes with clear self-stick paper. Let your children hang their shapes in a special place in the room each morning to let you know that they have arrived.

Musical Roll Call

953 Here's a different way to start your school day. When taking attendance, sing out each child's name and have the child respond by singing back his or her name exactly as you did.

Lining Up

No More Pushing

954 Paint or tape short, horizontal stripes on the floor leading to your drinking fountain. When the children form a line to get a drink, each child can stand on a stripe and move forward to the next stripe when it becomes free. This works well for the sink area too.

Lining Up at the Door

955 Place a strip of masking tape on the floor of your room about 5 feet from your door. When your children line up to go outside, have the first child stand with toes behind the tape strip. This will keep the children away from the door and allow you to open it easily.

Carpet Square Bridge

956 To make lining up more fun, try this. Make a long "bridge" by cutting carpet squares into strips and taping them together end to end. Place the bridge on the floor alongside a smiling paper alligator. Have your children walk in line on the bridge, being careful not to step off and let the alligator "nip" their toes.

Line-Up Time Fun

957 Copy favorite songs, poems and finger plays onto index cards. Group the cards by subject or season and place them in a file box by your door. Whenever your children are waiting in line to go out, you can select a card and do the activity on it with the group.

Moving From One Activity to Another

Moving by Concept

958 Have your children move from one activity to the other according to their shirt colors, types of shoes, numbers of buttons, etc.

Transition Cards

959 Decorate index cards with different shapes, numerals or letters. Give one card to each child. Have your children move from one place to another according to the items drawn on their cards.

Vehicle Moves

960 As your children move from one activity to another, have them pretend to be riding bicycles, flying airplanes, or sailing boats.

Animal Moves

961 Have your children pretend to swim like fish, fly like birds, or wiggle like worms as they move from one place to another.

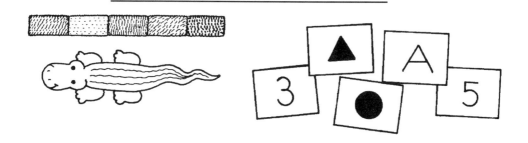

To the Playground

962 Ask your children to see how many different ways they can move to the playground. Encourage them to try hopping, skipping, dancing, and jumping.

Down the Hall

963 As you walk down a hall, have your children look for a particular color or count a particular item. Or have them count the number of steps.

Pretend Shoes

964 When moving from place to place, have your children pretend to walk in cowboy boots, leather moccasins, high heels, etc.

Grab a Cloud

965 Let your children pretend to reach up and grab clouds to ride on as they "float" from one activity to another. Have them let their clouds go back up into the sky when they arrive at each activity area.

How Quiet Can You Be?

966 As you move from one activity to another, recite the following chant with your children.

How quiet can you be

As you tiptoe after me?

I come to (the circle) without a sound,

I cross my legs and then sit down.

April Brown

Let's All Tiptoe

967 Recite the following chant as you move from place to place with your group.

Let's all tiptoe to (our circle),

Let's all tiptoe after me.

Let's all tiptoe to (our circle),

And see how quiet we can be.

April Brown

Musical Transitions

Tiptoe Tune

968 To help your children move to another area quietly and quickly, play a "tiptoe tune" on the upper keys of a piano. A tape recording of similar music also works well.

From Loud to Soft

969 Play music as your children move from one activity to another. Start by playing loud and fast. Then gradually play softer and more slowly until all the children are seated in the desired area.

Transition Time Song

970 Sing the song below at transition times, substituting the names of your children where appropriate.

Sung to: "Twinkle, Twinkle, Little Star"

Joseph and Libby, come around,

Peter and Becky, sit on the ground.

Abby and Tommy will sit next to you,

Kerri, Billy and Kim will, too.

Andrew, Andrew is the last one,

Now we're ready to have some fun!

Krista Alworth

Join the Circle

971 Sing the following song with your children at transition times.

> Sung to: "Frere Jacques"

> Time to end play, time to end play,
> Let's clean up, let's clean up.
> Then we'll join the circle,
> Then we'll join the circle,
> For more fun, for more fun.

> *Melissa Leonard*

I Am Waiting

972 Sing this song when you want your children to quiet down between activities.

> Sung to: "Frere Jacques"

> I am waiting, I am waiting,
> For my group, for my group.
> Won't you please be quiet?
> Won't you please be quiet?
> Shh, shh, shh! Shh, shh, shh!

> *Helen Unterborn*

Nap Time

Labeling Blankets

973 Use fabric paint pens to label nap-time blankets with your teaching center's name. The fabric pens will give a pretty, handcrafted look to the blankets.

Nap-Time Necklaces

974 Cut small seasonal shapes from construction paper and string them on loops of yarn to make necklaces. When a child rests quietly during nap time, write "(Child's name) took a great nap" on a necklace and let the child wear it home. Not only will the necklaces serve as good incentives, they'll also let parents know that their children have had naps.

Sweet Dreams

975 If children have difficulty settling down at nap time, place drops of their parents' cologne on their pillows. The familiar scents will help soothe the children and make resting easier. Store the pillows in separate plastic bags when not in use.

Rock-A-Bye Babies

976 To help active children settle down at rest time, encourage them to put their own "babies" to sleep. Each child can rock or cuddle a favorite doll or a stuffed toy and sing it a lullaby.

Quieting Down

Clapping Rhythms

977 To help your children quiet down between activities, clap a rhythm for them to copy. Start by clapping loud, then clap softer and softer until finally your hands are resting in your lap.

Counting Fun

978 When your children need a few minutes to settle down after an active time, have them sit quietly and close their eyes. Tell them that together you are going to count to 10 or 20, then start the counting. Not only will your children get a short rest, they'll also be practicing their math skills. And they'll know exactly when quiet time will be over.

Whisper Game

979 When you want the group to quiet down between activities, try this. Tell your children that when they hear you whisper their names, they may go on to the next activity. Remind them that they must be very quiet in order to hear your voice.

Classical Cool Down

980 Choose a recording of a slow, soothing piece of classical music. Tell your children that whenever they hear the music being played, it's time to quiet down. This works especially well when a bouncy activity precedes a quiet one.

Special Toy Time

981 For a quiet-down activity, let each child play on a separate baby blanket with a container of small toys that are different from those in general use. Since the toys are special and the children don't have to share, this activity will provide a welcome relief from the usual classroom routine.

Signals for Transition

Verbal Signal

982 Shortly before a transition, tell your children what they will be doing and when. For instance, you might say, "When the big hand of the clock is on five, we will stop playing our game and go outside."

Rolling a Ball

983 When you want your children to stop what they are doing and gather in a particular area of the room, roll a large ball to a child who is already there. Have the child call out his or her name and then roll the ball back to you. When the other children see and hear this signal, they will respond quickly in order to get their turns too.

Blinking Lights Signal

984 Turn your room lights off and on whenever you want your children to stop what they are doing and listen.

Arms Up

985 Here's an easy signal for getting your group's attention. Teach your children that whenever they see you hold up your arm, they are to quiet down and raise one arm too. The first few children to respond to your signal will alert the others to follow suit.

Transition Flag

986 Make a group flag with your children. Each day, let a different child be in charge of the flag, waving it high to signal the end of one activity and the beginning of another.

Traffic Light Signal

987 Decorate a large milk carton to resemble a traffic light. Make movable flaps to cover the three "lights." Explain to your children that when the green light is showing, it means continue an activity; when the yellow light is showing, it means start cleaning up; and when the red light is showing, it means stop and listen.

Transition Time Activities

Nurture Nature

988 Give each child a plant with his or her name on it to place on a windowsill. Let your children "nurture nature" during transition times by watering, dusting and talking to their plants.

Wiggle Game

989 During transition times, have your children wiggle their bodies from head to toe. Then have them stop, place their hands in their laps, and listen.

Pocket Chart Fun

990 On small cards, write (or illustrate) brief activities such as "Hum a favorite song" or "Find something yellow." Insert the cards in a pocket chart. When your children need things to do during transition times, they can use the activity cards.

Playing Games

991 A fun way to pass transition times is to play games such as Simon Says, I Spy, or I'm Thinking of Something. You can start a game and then let your children take turns being the leader.

Feeding the Birds

992 Save crumbs from snack time and let your children take them outside to feed the birds. This is a great transition activity, and you'll be recycling the crumbs too.

Let's Pretend

993 Here are some fun things for your children to do during transition times: pretend to lock their lips and put the keys in their pockets; pretend to be bowls of gelatin and shake all over; pretend to put on magic ears for listening.

Mystery Egg

994 Secretly fill a large, plastic egg with an edible treat or a small toy. At transition time, let each child shake the egg and try guessing what's inside. When the egg is finally opened, let everyone enjoy the treat inside.

What's Next?

995 Cut little window flaps in a piece of paper. At transition time, place the paper over a picture of an activity that your children will be doing next. As the children open one window flap at a time, have them guess what that activity will be.

Mystery Bag

996 At transition time, hide in a bag an object that identifies the next activity you have planned. Let your children reach into the bag, identify the object by touch, and guess what the next activity will be.

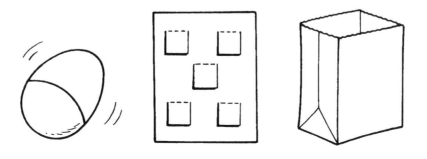

When Day Is Done

Going Home Rhyme

997 End your school day with a made-up rhyme like the one that follows.

> Now our day is done,
>
> We've all had lots of fun.
>
> Tomorrow is another day,
>
> And we'll be coming back to play.

Kerry L. Stanley

What Did You Do Today?

998 When parents ask their children what they did at school, the answer they often get is "I don't know." To avoid this, have your children sit with you near the day's end. Ask, "What was your favorite activity today?" Write down each child's response on a large piece of paper. Review all the responses before the children leave for home.

Going Home Box

999 Place a "going home box" by your door to hold stray belongings found throughout the day. Children and parents can check the box as they leave.

Year's End

Memory Book

1000 Near the end of the school year, let each child tell you about an activity or a time at school that he or she particularly enjoyed. Write down the children's responses on separate pieces of paper for them to illustrate. Then put all the papers together to make a memory book for your reading corner.

Graduation Art Display

1001 Throughout the school year, save pieces of artwork that your children have done. At graduation time, display each child's work along with a photo of the child standing beside an easel and holding a palette and a paintbrush. If desired, have each child wear an artist's beret when you take the picture.

Index

Index

Index

Contributor Acknowledgements

Many of the tips in this book were submitted by *Totline* newsletter readers. We wish to acknowledge the following contributors.

Cathryn Abraham, St. Charles, IL
Carol W. Adams, Clinton, MD
Krista Alworth, Verona, NJ
Sr. Roberta Bailey, Dade City, FL
Betty Ruth Baker, Waco, TX
Julie Bakerlis, Dudley, MA
Jacqueline Bakker, Sinking Spring, PA
Denise Bedell, Westland, MI
Ellen Bedford, Bridgeport, CT
Marcia Berquist, Virginia, MN
Lynn Beverly, Somerset, NJ
Sr. Mary Bezold, Melbourne, KY
John Bittinger, Everett, WA
Fannie Blackledge, Heath, OH
Ricke A. Bly, Tyler, MN
Janice Bodenstedt, Jackson, MI
Kim Bohl, Adrian, MI
April Brown, Barnesville, PA
Reva Bucholtz, Tucson, AZ
Deb Cech, Mt. Penn, PA
Mary Cheetham, Santa Ana, CA
Joanie Christian, Everett, WA
Tamara Clohessy, Eureka, CA
Jenifer Contaya, Arlington, TX
June Crow, Weaverville, NC
Kim Davids, Buffalo Center, IA
Sheryl Davids, Buffalo Center, IA
Lynn Davis, Macungie, PA
Suzanne L. Davis, Robinson, PA
Suzanne Day, Fleetwood, PA
Marjorie Debowy, Stony Brook, NY
Marcia Dedenbach, Hawthorne, FL
Kelley Del Rossi, Downington, PA
Christine Deren, Kutztown, PA
Debbie Deverell, Denver, CO
Joyce DeVilbiss, Silver Spring, MD
Cindy Dingwall, Palatine, IL
Elisabetta DiStravolo, West Reading, PA
Lona DiTommaso, Oceanside, NY
Maribeth Donnelly, Kunkletown, PA

Elaine Dufner, Southampton, PA
Kelly Eagle, Fleetwood, PA
Laura Egge, Lake Oswego, OR
Ruth Engle, Kirkland, WA
Bronwen Evans, Reading, PA
Susan Fell, Cedar Knolls, NJ
Karen Focht, Reading, PA
Susan Foster, Lenhartsville, PA
Kristi Franseen, Poplar Grove, IL
Susan Fronheiser, Bally, PA
Rita Galloway, Harlingen, TX
Mary Lou Gathings, Cathedral City, CA
Tracy Goheen, Dauberville, PA
Cathy B. Griffith, Plainsboro, NJ
Lanette Gutierrez, Olympia, WA
Rene Gutyan, Williams Lake, B.C.
Peggy Hanley, St. Joseph, MI
Nancy Hartman, Fleetwood, PA
Nancy J. Heimark, Grand Forks, ND
Diane Hemplemann, Johnsburg, IL
Susan Henry, Rickreall, OR
Jane Hensley, Kent, OH
Cynthia Holt, Danbury, CT
Sally J. Horton, Waukegan, IL
Erma Hunt, Winston-Salem, NC
Joan Hunter, Elbridge, NY
Melode Hurst, Grand Junction, CO
Barbara Jackson, Denton, TX
Ellen Javernick, Loveland, CO
Debbie Jones, Las Vegas, NV
Megata Jones, Columbus, OH
Laura Jordan, Pittsfield, MA
Melissa Keck, Oswego, IL
Kimberly Kenney, Lansdown, PA
Barbara Kingsley, Flushing, NY
Agnes Kirchgasler, Salt Lake City, UT
Peggy Klasse, Westbrook, MN
Cindy Kostoff, Findlay, OH
Neoma Kreuter, Upland, CA
Elaine Kropp, Oakmont, PA

Judith Lahore, Mercer Island, WA
Vicky Lane, Lansdowne, PA
Judy Laureano, Reading, PA
Teresa Lemmon, Sedalia, MO
Melissa Leonard, Minersville, PA
Beverly Lowthert, Kutztown, PA
Carol J. Luckenbill, Bernville, PA
Nancy MacDonald, Wallingford, PA
Lisa Marie Martin, Allentown, PA
Gina Masci, Arlington, MA
Barb Mazzochi, Willa Park, IL
Kathy McCullough, Everett, WA
Jan McGilloway, Flourtown, PA
Patricia McKinnon, Seattle, WA
Richard McKinnon, Seattle, WA
Joleen Meier, Marietta, GA
Lynn Meyers, Pittsfield, MA
Susan A. Miller, Kutztown, PA
Angel Nearhouse, Allentown, PA
Linnae Newman, Reading, PA
Jane M. Niehls, Barto, PA
Ann M. O'Connell, Coaldale, PA
Michele O'Donnell, Doyelestown, PA
Lois Olson, Webster City, IA
Sharon Olson, Minot, ND
Trudy Palko, Metuchen, NJ
Susan M. Paprocki, Northbrook, IL
Susan Peters, Upland, CA
Maxine Pincott, Windsor, CT
Eleanor Pini, Seattle, WA
Ruth Prall, Sterling, CO
Lois E. Putnam, Pilot Mt., NC
Beverly Qualheim, Marquette, MI
Pat Reinik, Reading, PA
Vicki Reynolds, East Hanover, NJ
Jane Roake, Oswego, IL
Christine Robertson, Oakmont, PA
Deborah Roessel, Flemington, NJ
Kathy Rogaway, Palo Alto, CA
Frankie Lyn Roman, Reading, PA
Sue Schliecker, Waukesha, WI
Susan Schoelkopf, Rochester, VA
Debbie Scofield, Niceville, FL
Lois T. Scofield, Spokane, WA
Marion Scofield, Spokane, WA
Michelle Sears, Glen Falls, NY
Karen Seehusen, Ft. Dodge, IA

Donna Shaw, Hollidaysburg, PA
Judy Sheppard-Segal, Falmouth, ME
Betty Silkunas, Lansdale, PA
Debbie Sipola, Hales Corner, WI
Kathy Sizer, Tustin, CA
Paulette M. Skinner, Reading, PA
Janet Sloey, Manchester, MO
Beth Smalley, Celina, OH
Jacki Smallwood, Royersford, PA
Rosemary Spatafora, Pleasant Ridge, MI
Kerry Stanley, Centre Square, PA
Mary Sterling, Jacksonville, FL
Jackie Stevison, St. Louis, MO
Diane Thom, Maple Valley, WA
Suzanne Thompson, Whittier, CA
Kathleen Tobey, Griffith, IN
Betty Turman, Reading, PA
Helen Unterborn, Kendall, NJ
Michele L. Urich, Sellersville, PA
Brenda Valenzuela, Ft. Worth, TX
Lucia Vietro, Mountainside, NJ
Leslie Wagner, Fredonia, NY
Gayle Walrath, Kutztown, PA
Susan Walsh, Kutztown, PA
Cheri L. Waters, Horsham, PA
Debbie Watson, Little Rock, AR
Gail Weidner, Tustin, CA
Nancy C. Windes, Denver, CO
Pat Witman, Reading, PA
Peggy Wolf, Pittsburgh, PA
Yosie Yoshimura, Gardena, CA
Maryann Zucker, Reno, NV

Totline® PUBLICATIONS

Teacher Resources

ART SERIES
Ideas for successful art experiences.
Cooperative Art
Special Day Art
Outdoor Art

BEST OF TOTLINE® SERIES
Totline's best ideas.
Best of Totline Newsletter
Best of Totline Bear Hugs
Best of Totline Parent Flyers

BUSY BEES SERIES
Seasonal ideas for twos and threes.
Fall • Winter • Spring • Summer

CELEBRATIONS SERIES
Early learning through celebrations.
Small World Celebrations
Special Day Celebrations
Great Big Holiday Celebrations
Celebrating Likes and Differences

CIRCLE TIME SERIES
Put the spotlight on circle time!
Introducing Concepts at Circle Time
Music and Dramatics at Circle Time
Storytime Ideas for Circle Time

EMPOWERING KIDS SERIES
Positive solutions to behavior issues.
Can-Do Kids
Problem-Solving Kids

EXPLORING SERIES
Versatile, hands-on learning.
Exploring Sand • Exploring Water

FOUR SEASONS
Active learning through the year.
Art • Math • Movement • Science

JUST RIGHT PATTERNS
8-page, reproducible pattern folders.
Valentine's Day • St. Patrick's Day •
Easter • Halloween • Thanksgiving •
Hanukkah • Christmas • Kwanzaa •
Spring • Summer • Autumn •
Winter • Air Transportation • Land
Transportation • Service Vehicles
• Water Transportation • Train
• Desert Life • Farm Life • Forest
Life • Ocean Life • Wetland Life
• Zoo Life • Prehistoric Life

KINDERSTATION SERIES
Learning centers for kindergarten.
Calculation Station
Communication Station
Creation Station
Investigation Station

1•2•3 SERIES
Open-ended learning.
Art • Blocks • Games • Colors •
Puppets • Reading & Writing •
Math • Science • Shapes

1001 SERIES
Super reference books.
1001 Teaching Props
1001 Teaching Tips
1001 Rhymes & Fingerplays

PIGGYBACK® SONG BOOKS
New lyrics sung to favorite tunes!
Piggyback Songs
More Piggyback Songs
Piggyback Songs for Infants
and Toddlers
Holiday Piggyback Songs
Animal Piggyback Songs
Piggyback Songs for School
Piggyback Songs to Sign
Spanish Piggyback Songs
More Piggyback Songs for School

PROJECT BOOK SERIES
*Reproducible, cross-curricular project
books and project ideas.*
Start With Art
Start With Science

REPRODUCIBLE RHYMES
*Make-and-take-home books for
emergent readers.*
Alphabet Rhymes • Object Rhymes

SNACKS SERIES
Nutrition combines with learning.
Super Snacks • Healthy Snacks •
Teaching Snacks • Multicultural Snacks

TERRIFIC TIPS
Handy resources with valuable ideas.
Terrific Tips for Directors
Terrific Tips for Toddler Teachers
Terrific Tips for Preschool Teachers

THEME-A-SAURUS® SERIES
Classroom-tested, instant themes.
Theme-A-Saurus
Theme-A-Saurus II
Toddler Theme-A-Saurus
Alphabet Theme-A-Saurus
Nursery Rhyme Theme-A-Saurus
Storytime Theme-A-Saurus
Multisensory Theme-A-Saurus
Transportation Theme-A-Saurus
Field Trip Theme-A-Saurus

TODDLER RESOURCES
Great for working with 18 mos–3 yrs.
Playtime Props for Toddlers
Toddler Art

Parent Resources

A YEAR OF FUN SERIES
Age-specific books for parenting.
Just for Babies • Just for Ones •
Just for Twos • Just for Threes •
Just for Fours • Just for Fives

LEARN WITH PIGGYBACK® SONGS
*Captivating music with
age-appropriate themes.*
Songs & Games for…
Babies • Toddlers • Threes • Fours
Sing a Song of…
Letters • Animals • Colors • Holidays
• Me • Nature • Numbers

LEARN WITH STICKERS
*Beginning workbook and first reader
with 100-plus stickers.*
Balloons • Birds • Bows • Bugs •
Butterflies • Buttons • Eggs • Flags •
Flowers • Hearts • Leaves • Mittens

MY FIRST COLORING BOOK
*White illustrations on black back-
grounds—perfect for toddlers!*
All About Colors
All About Numbers
Under the Sea
Over and Under
Party Animals
Tops and Bottoms

PLAY AND LEARN
Activities for learning through play.
Blocks • Instruments • Kitchen
Gadgets • Paper • Puppets • Puzzles

RAINY DAY FUN
*This activity book for parent-child fun
keeps minds active on rainy days!*

RHYME & REASON STICKER WORKBOOKS
*Sticker fun to boost
language development and
thinking skills.*
Up in Space
All About Weather
At the Zoo
On the Farm
Things That Go
Under the Sea

SEEDS FOR SUCCESS
*Ideas to help children develop
essential life skills for future success.*
Growing Creative Kids
Growing Happy Kids
Growing Responsible Kids
Growing Thinking Kids

THEME CALENDARS
Activities for every day.
Toddler Theme Calendar
Preschool Theme Calendar
Kindergarten Theme Calendar

TIME TO LEARN
Ideas for hands-on learning.
Colors • Letters • Measuring •
Numbers • Science • Shapes •
Matching and Sorting • New Words
• Cutting and Pasting •
Drawing and Writing • Listening •
Taking Care of Myself

Posters
Celebrating Childhood Posters
Reminder Posters

Puppet Pals
Instant puppets!
Children's Favorites • The Three Bears
• Nursery Rhymes • Old MacDonald
• More Nursery Rhymes • Three
Little Pigs • Three Billy Goats Gruff •
Little Red Riding Hood

Manipulatives
CIRCLE PUZZLES
African Adventure Puzzle

LITTLE BUILDER STACKING CARDS
Castle • The Three Little Pigs

Tot-Mobiles
*Each set includes four punch-out,
easy-to-assemble mobiles.*
Animals & Toys
Beginning Concepts
Four Seasons

**Start right,
start bright!**

Totline products are available at parent and teacher stores.